A Good Red gerree   p 32
   Poulet au riz   p 50
A Good Irish stew
Royal Russian S...
Filet de Sole Veronique   p 69
Cream dressing   p 71
Brown bread ice cream   p 107
Kipper souffle   p 121
Pheasant Normande   p 123   (a fairly
                                  good version!)
Chocolate mousse   p 124   Glenfiddich
  Cardinal pears   p 125
Spinach terrine   p 160
Champagne dindu   p 70

BY ROYAL INVITATION

BY ROYAL INVITATION

UNITY HALL AND
INGRID SEWARD

SIDGWICK & JACKSON
LONDON

First published in 1988 by
Sidgwick & Jackson Limited
1 Tavistock Chambers, Bloomsbury Way
London WC1A 2SG

ISBN 0 283 99704 4

Typeset by Rowland Phototypesetting Limited
Bury St Edmunds, Suffolk
Printed by Butler & Tanner Limited
Frome and London

CONTENTS

ILLUSTRATIONS

1

ROYAL STYLE

The British Royal Family are probably the richest and most privileged people in the world. I use the word 'probably' only because the Queen's wealth is untold and her vast financial assets are never disclosed to the nation she heads. And since she pays no income tax, the growth rate must be mind-boggling.

The family live in a collection of castles and palaces, surrounded by an incredible number of the treasures of Britain. Many of these treasures they do not own, but they have the day-to-day use and pleasure of them. The family are waited on hand and foot by a huge staff of servants – at the summer holiday in Balmoral there will be around 120 staff to wait on perhaps a dozen people – though, to be fair, the Royal Family never use the word 'servant', considering it demeaning. They call those who work for them in a domestic capacity 'staff'.

The policemen, chauffeurs, pages and older, long-serving staff are all called by their surnames. Footmen, valets and dressers are called by their christian names. The family are most definitely Your Majesty (the Queen and the Queen Mother), Your Royal Highness, or Sir and Ma'am. Everyone who works for them has a definite function, and the end result is cosseting the royals. One of Prince Philip's valet's duties was to put the toothpaste on his toothbrush every night and morning before the Duke cleaned his teeth.

On a higher level than the staff, the group of distinguished people known as the Household deal with all the money matters and paying of bills. It is possible that neither the Queen nor Prince Charles has ever signed a cheque. One recent change is that, though Prince Charles and Princess Diana would not carry a credit card, members of their Household do. Sir John Riddell, Prince Charles's private secretary, now carries a Duchy of Cornwall American Express card, as does Anne Beckwith-Smith, Diana's chief lady-in-waiting. In this they have only just caught up with the rest of us – though royalty have had car telephones for years for security purposes.

For all their vast wealth, the Royal Family do not lead lives of extravagant Hollywood luxury. They rarely travel for pleasure. They are at their happiest in the Highlands of Scotland where they spend their ten weeks of summer holiday, or in chilly Sandringham in Norfolk where they spend six weeks in the winter. But actually they are content anywhere in the country surrounded by horses and dogs; they like to shoot and fish. The newest addition to their ranks, the Duchess of York, who to the popular press will be forever Fergie, is happy in these surroundings, something that helped to qualify her as a suitable royal bride. Only the younger members of the family can be found on ski slopes and on tropical islands. Neither holiday venue is the Queen or Prince Philip's style.

With the exception of Diana, Fergie and Princess Michael of Kent, royal women are uninterested in fashion. They spend their own money as if every penny were their last. They have no snobbery at all about their ordinary subjects, but they believe that many of the richest of the British aristocracy are 'too grand for us'.

In their dealings with people they rarely put a foot wrong once they have grown up. The Duke of York, Prince Edward and The Princess Royal all began by taking after their father, Prince Philip, whose public manner left a great deal to be desired in his youth and still often does. The royal children's manners *are* inbuilt from childhood, by Nanny, but in the days of rebellious youth it takes a while for Nanny's training to come through. Only Prince Charles has never really received a tut-tut press for his youthful peccadilloes.

However, if they are going to involve themselves in a deb's delight-type teenage rumpus it is usually with their own kind and in private. Prince Charles once left his valet a note telling him to ask the chef to make two big catering tubs of custard. He wanted them ready by five o'clock as he was going to take them to Lady Sarah Keswick's very grand home, where she then lived with her parents, in London's Holland Park. Lady Sarah is an old friend of his, and he is now godfather to one of her children. The chef was not told what the custard was for. It all had to be handled very discreetly, as Lady

Sarah was going to have a custard pie fight at her house. Unfortunately, the pastry chef cooked a superb custard, thinking it was for eating – not throwing. The Prince transported the two tubs, still very warm, in the back of his Range Rover. And when it was thrown it had still not cooled. It made the most appalling mess. Lady Keswick's father, Lord Dalhousie, the Queen Mother's treasurer and friend, was furious. The dining room had to be entirely redecorated. And it was the most terrible waste of a good custard.

But this rather juvenile party only happened in the cosy confines of their own set. And apart from the occasional outbreak – for which who can blame them? – in private, the Royal Family have an old-fashioned, easy-going style. Their aim is to be comfortable themselves and to see that the people around them are equally comfortable and at their ease.

Prince Charles is always particularly concerned that, when in public, those around him are not embarrassed. A few years ago he went to a function given for a third world leader. Suddenly the guest of honour began to drink from his finger bowl. There was a faint murmur of giggling around the table and a few nudges. Prince Charles, seeing what was happening, picked up his finger bowl and did exactly the same. The gigglers then shamefacedly followed suit.

Back at the Palace and in private, the Royal Family do sometimes laugh at these gaffes of the hoi-polloi. One of Princess Diana's oft-told family stories concerns attending a James Bond film premiere. It took place before the wedding, when she was still Lady Diana. She was seated next to the star of the movie, Roger Moore, who, every time he turned to speak to her, surreptitiously sprayed himself with Gold Spot mouth freshener. The Princess was quite aware of what was going on as she could hear the little hiss of the spray and smell the pepperminty scent of the stuff.

She pretended not to notice, because most of the Royal Family would feel they had failed in their duty if they embarrassed anybody. They practise the simple courtesies of never being late and never forgetting names. Of course, they are very carefully briefed with people's names, particularly if it is someone whom they have met before. Also, their equerries and ladies-in-waiting are trained to soothe people's nerves before being presented to the Queen, because people do get very nervous. It's rare for anyone presented to Her Majesty to be able to remember what she said once she has moved on.

Their good manners are not just for the public. The Royal Family do not use four-letter words. Prince Philip has been known to shout at people, and the word 'bloody' figures in his vocabulary. 'Bloody' is also Prince Charles's strongest expletive. The Queen's strongest word is 'fool', but shouting at people is not one of her habits, nor Prince Charles's, nor, most certainly, the Queen Mother's.

However, while the Queen shows respect to her subjects, she is equally punctilious about the way that people approach her and her family. She insists that none of the centuries-old rules on dealing with the monarchy is ever broken – not out of any feeling of personal grandeur, but because she is the embodiment of the Crown, and respect must always be shown to the Crown. No one sits in the Queen's presence without being invited to do so. She always enters a room first, and in public takes the head of the table. There are only a handful of people in the world who call her by her christian name.

Some of these formalities do cause some difficulty on occasions. One unwritten and very awkward rule about dining with the Queen is that, once seated, no one is supposed to leave the table until she does. It is considered very bad form to leap up and head for the gents or ladies in the middle of the meal. Nature must be attended to before sitting down. There was one occasion at Sandringham when, following tradition, the local clergyman who was to preach at the weekend was invited to join the family for dinner. Deeply embarrassed, he explained to the Queen's equerry that he would like very much to be present, but that he suffered from a very weak bladder and might well have to excuse himself during dinner. The Queen instantly relayed a message that this was of no consequence and everyone would quite understand. However, she mentioned the parson's difficulty to no one else, feeling that his health problems were nobody's business but his own.

The first time he excused himself from the table over dinner nobody said a word, except for Princess Margaret who looked around the table and said, puzzled, 'Where's he going?'

No one answered her.

The second time he went she said in outraged tones, believing he was slighting her sister: 'What *is* he up to?'

'Do be quiet,' the Queen said. 'He's going to the loo.'

It was such an unusual thing to happen that the other guests couldn't help staring at the poor man when he tried to slip back unobtrusively into his place. So should you ever dine with the Queen, remember not to drink too much and to pay a quick visit before you sit down to eat.

The Queen is terribly superstitious about the number thirteen. If there are unexpectedly thirteen for a meal (if the clergyman is invited rather late in the day, which does happen sometimes, or if someone is unavoidably delayed), the dining table will be laid up for only ten. At one end another smaller table will be laid for three, with a three- or four-inch gap separating it from the main table. So in effect there are two tables, one for three and one for ten.

Even if there is only one person present who is not a member of the family, protocol would demand not only that no one would leave the table while the Queen was sitting, but that she should take the head of the table, that no one would sit before she sat, and that she would be served first. In private, she always gives these honours to her husband. Interestingly, both the Queen and Prince Philip insist that the Queen Mother is treated as number one guest and served first when she is present on family occasions. And they prefer round tables, which solve any protocol problems.

The Royal Family always go to enormous lengths to find out what their guests prefer to eat, and on any large occasion they play safe with the simplest of meals. After all, it's not everyone who enjoys snipe on toast for breakfast, as Prince Philip does – particularly when he has shot it himself. They like their hosts to be equally careful. There are rare occasions when Prince Charles and Princess Diana will be staying in someone's home and their hosts don't take the trouble to find out in advance what their tastes in food are. But like any polite guest, all members of the Royal Family will eat what is put in front of them.

Prince Charles dislikes chocolate in any form when served as a pudding (though he does like chocolate Bath Olivers), and it is astonishing how often chocolate mousse, chocolate cake or chocolate sauces are served to him. When served snake in Hong Kong, the Prince ate it and muttered quietly: 'The things I do for England.' It's not surprising that he himself says he has a cast-iron stomach.

'When I ate raw squid in Japan,' he once said, 'it tasted like chopped up garden hose. We ate very strange food in the Far East: things like octopus. But the sight of all those suckers was rather revolting. I wouldn't like the idea of sheep's eyes . . . maybe if I could swallow them in one go! It is probably the thought of having to chew them that puts me off. But I'm quite prepared to try anything once.'

Even so, all they ask is that people ask questions first – and it's quite simple. Should Charles and Diana be coming to a meal at your home, the routine is to ring up the Prince's private office and ask for guidance on what not to serve.

The Royal Family always get it right for their guests. When the Chief Rabbi came to lunch at the Palace, he insisted on bringing his own kosher chef, much to the Palace chef's annoyance. The man was brought from a Jewish restaurant in London's Soho and, apart from cooking, he personally had to serve the Rabbi. Without making any fuss about security, the Queen permitted him to come into the dining room. It is hard to imagine many other countries allowing a complete stranger into the presence of their head of state. The Queen simply accepted the situation on religious grounds, as she does with Arab guests and their different customs. She continues to serve alcohol at banquets when she has guests from Islamic countries, but they are not expected to drink it. Jugs of orange juice are always placed by them at table. What they drink in their own rooms is their own business, but in front of the world, at the Queen's banquet, they can be seen to be drinking fruit juice.

Guests at the Palace are always left a small drinks tray in their room. This holds three small decanters – one each of gin, sherry and scotch – plus mixers and mineral waters. Some of the Arab guests empty the tray as quickly as anyone else. Not that the Queen ever inquires; but the staff spot that the alcohol has gone.

Some of the requests that the Royal Family receive from their guests do create small difficulties. When Emperor Hirohito of Japan came for a state visit his actual food was enough of a problem, but an even bigger one was that it all had to be served tepid. As the entire system at the Palace is dedicated to serving hot food, this was not easy to achieve. In the end the silver dishes containing his food were left out of the hot plate and allowed to cool down naturally.

Many people imagine that the Queen and her family live on caviare, foie gras and champagne. In fact, nothing could be further from the truth. The Royal Family do not spend their money lightly on great delicacies, nor does one hear or see many champagne corks popping about their palaces. In an effort not to appear extravagant, they have even cut out champagne at diplomatic receptions. Guests would not be disappointed in the food that the Queen serves, but they might be surprised at its simplicity.

This is not to say that the Royal Family do not enjoy the opportunity of eating the kind of foods that they never buy for themselves. The huge biscuit tin-sized container of caviare that the late Shah of Persia sent to the Queen every December as a New Year's present was regarded as a great treat. The Queen would save it for a first course when there were fourteen sitting down to dine at the Sandringham winter holiday. The caviare was served in its tin, placed in a silver bowl and set into another bowl of crushed ice. The chef would prepare toast, chopped onion and chopped hard-boiled egg with muslin-wrapped chunks of lemon to eat with this extravagant delicacy. Each guest had a heaped tablespoonful, and every mouthful would have cost the Shah about £50. There were never any leftovers!

Lord Mountbatten, Prince Philip's uncle who was murdered by the IRA, was also a recipient of Iran's generosity. Every New Year the Iranian ambassador would send him a similar tin, which he kept upstairs at his home, Broadlands, in Hampshire. His special favourites – his granddaughter, Amanda Knatchbull, and Prince Charles – would be invited upstairs for a secret feast before lunch.

For the rest of the year the Palace never saw caviare. And since the death of the Shah, it is never served at all. The Queen would not dream of buying it for herself. As it happens, she buys little for herself anyway. The Royal Family are astonishingly self-sufficient. They catch their own salmon, and shoot their own game and venison. They raise their own chickens and turkeys for Christmas, and cut the Christmas trees for the Palace and Windsor from their own pine forests at Windsor and Sandringham. They eat their own free-range eggs and their own fresh vegetables, grown all the year round on the royal farms. The Royal Family never eat anything tinned or frozen. Their staff, on the other hand, do. What is fresh is saved for the family.

They grow their own flowers in the greenhouses at Windsor, where they also have their own mushroom farm. But many of these activities are mainly business ventures, something that the Duke often fails to remember if he asks for mushrooms and the chef says he hasn't any in the kitchen.

'What do you mean?' the Duke shouts. 'There's acres of them out there!'

The chefs do suffer from the Duke's wrath. On one occasion the Duke had been visiting in Windsor Great Park, and he came home with two globe artichokes that he had been given. He decided they would make a perfect light supper for himself and the Queen, and so they were sent down to the kitchen to the young chef who was on duty. Normally artichokes are served as a separate course at the Palace – they call them a dressed vegetable. So the young chef took all the leaves off, threw them away and just cooked the hearts. These arrived beautifully presented under a silver cover, but there wasn't a great deal left to present. The Duke was not amused.

All the produce from the farms in Windsor Great Park and at Sandringham goes to the market, and some of it comes back into the kitchen – retail. In any case some items, like blackcurrants, are produced in such quantities that the Royal Family couldn't possibly eat them all themselves. At Sandringham they grow their own delicious peaches, a much sought after delicacy and definitely reserved for the family. Boxes of mangoes, a great favourite of Prince Philip's, are sent to them regularly by the Indian government, and the mangoes, like the caviare, are always served on a bed of ice. When Prince Charles went to India he brought back six of these fruits for his father. The Queen is traditionally offered any sturgeon caught in her waters, and all the swans in Britain belong to the monarch. Her Majesty's ancestor, Queen Elizabeth I, was fond of swan pie, but no one eats them nowadays.

All the milk and cream that the Royal Family drink comes from the Windsor dairy herd. The cream is dispatched to wherever the Royal Family happen to be each night, even as far away as Scotland. It is marvellous milk and cream, untreated and very thick. The cream is packaged in its own special cardboard carton impressed with the royal cipher, while the milk comes in the royal milk bottle, with the royal stamp printed on it in blue. The Queen loses dozens of these bottles every year when people take them for souvenirs. At table, milk is always served in a silver jug. Another version of the royal milk bottle – screw-topped ones for picnics – still bear the royal cipher on the side.

Any meat and fish they buy comes from London's food markets, where they have a deal with the retailer. If they forget something vital – or, rather, if the chef does – he rings up Harrods, who send it round by van.

The Queen chooses the day's meals from what is called the 'menu book'. This is a small, leather-bound red book with a pencil that runs through the front which also acts like a latch. The book contains the chef's suggestions, which he inscribes in his best handwriting and his best French every morning before the book is presented to Her Majesty by her page. She uses the book for guidance to decide the meals for the day, crossing out the dishes she doesn't fancy. Breakfast is the only meal of the day in which the chef has a totally free hand. Menus for all other meals are always chosen by the Queen herself.

They have funny rules about fruit. It's served at Windsor, but not at the Palace except at breakfast. When served, it is always the last course, after the cheese, and called dessert. If the Queen is lunching alone upstairs she always has fruit on her own table. At Balmoral or Sandringham she never serves fruit at lunch, saving it for dinner, though a fruit bowl is always on the breakfast table to be eaten without any pomp. Guests take a knife and an apple and get on with it. At dinner, the eating of fruit becomes a great ritual involving a special dessert service – gilt knives, forks and spoons, and crystal finger bowls.

Prince Philip and his family turn the eating of a piece of fruit into an art form. The Duke will take the 'lid' from the ripe pear and gently scoop out the flesh until by the time he has finished all that is left is the skin, with the lid placed at the side. They cut all soft fruit round with a smooth-edged gilt knife, twist them and then take the stone out, before peeling. Bananas are avoided because they are too filling. When eating grapes, which are always included in the fruit bowl, they take the pips and skin from their mouths very discreetly. The grapes will have been washed in the kitchen and are cut with grape scissors. At their smaller homes, they just use ordinary paper scissors.

The only fish that they ever eat served with bones and all is the humble kipper, of which they are very fond. They take care when dealing with this fish, but for any other kind of fish it is as much as the chef's life is worth to leave in a bone. This did happen not once but twice, when the Queen Mother caught a fishbone in her throat. The first time was at Windsor when she was dining with her daughter. The second time she was eating at her home in Scotland, the Castle of Mey. On both occasions she had to be rushed to hospital. When the royal fishmonger who had supplied the offending sole at Windsor managed to apologize to her for the unfriendly action of his merchandise, she just laughed, wagged a finger and said: 'Don't let it happen again.'

The royal table manners are standard British: they eat with their knife in the right hand, the fork in the left. And most of them eat quite quickly. Prince Charles used to drive his father mad because he is such a slow eater. Normally the staff hand cream and sugar when it comes to serving the pudding, but because the Prince is so slow the footmen leave the jug and bowl beside him for when he gets round to it.

Surprisingly, the food at the Palace is sometimes not as good as a top restaurant would serve, which sends Prince Philip stamping off to the kitchen to give everyone hell. But then, providing food for the Royal Family is rather like running a restaurant and serving constantly varying numbers. At one time the Queen employed two head chefs – the royal chef and the staff chef. The royal chef cooked food for about twenty or thirty people, while the staff chef turned out 150 meals a day. Now there is only one kitchen where there used to be two. The old royal kitchen does duty for everyone, while the staff kitchen has been turned into what is known as the royal pastry where all the royal cakes, puddings, biscuits and so on are prepared.

Originally all the Palace head chefs were French, and French was spoken in the kitchen. Dating from the appointment of Ronald Aubery in 1937, the kitchens have been English-run and English is the language spoken in them.

Even today the royal chef never cooks for the staff. That less interesting chore is always left to the younger chefs, while the royal chef keeps an eye on what they are up to. But while the newer recruits are cooking under the supervision of the royal chef, they are being trained in royal style. All the chefs throughout the various royal homes have been promoted from being junior chefs at the Palace, where they have learned the cuisine that the Royal Family prefer.

This is a kind of moderated nouvelle cuisine – good ingredients, perfectly balanced, and attractive to the eye as well as to the palate. Every piece of food is cut to the same size. Each slice of carrot will match the next, each sauté potato will be of equal thickness and diameter. The little cubes of potato that the Royal Family enjoy deep-fried are all identical. The food is carefully decorated with greenery or piped sauces – no piece of fish is ever served ungarnished. All the food is prepared by hand, except for mayonnaises and mousses, for which a blender is used.

For state banquets the chef brings in extra help, mostly from the royal yacht if *Britannia* is in Britain. The naval cooks know the royal routine because when the Queen is at sea she takes her chefs to organize the cooking in the *Britannia*'s galley. If the Buckingham Palace kitchens are very busy indeed they call upon the retired chefs, who come with great good will – the work tops up their pensions. Everything is done without any stampede or panic.

The Royal Family have a quite amazing facility for avoiding embarrassing moments, and an equally great gift for ignoring those that do break the even tenor of their lives. Many years ago a drunken footman, who had spent far too long in the staff canteen, dropped a huge silver tray of drinks with a resounding crash. It was just as the Queen was receiving her guests at a Palace reception. The Queen and the Duke appeared to have neither seen nor heard what had happened as the crystal went crashing down, though the noise caused a momentary hush among the guests present.

These days the Palace does take precautions. The free staff drinks that are given on special occasions – the staff always get a drink at times like the announcement of a royal engagement – are given once they have finished their work, if not the following day.

Everything is done perfectly, as might be expected. Even the table napkins are specially folded in a number of different ways. The Prince of Wales feathers is one favourite design, but the pantry staff whose job it is to concentrate on the napkins can also make shoes (in which to sit an avocado), flowers, hats – anything that comes to mind. Some of the napkins do end up awfully creased when they are opened, though.

Special groups of people are responsible for setting tables. The silver pantry do their part and the china pantry the rest; then the cellarman supplies the water and the wine, and the coffee room the coffee at the end of the meal. Taking into account the chef who cooks the food, and the footman who serves it, a whole gang of people have been involved in what might be a simple little meal before the Queen has even picked up a bread stick.

The staff are very much part of the pageantry of royalty in that they have a series of different liveries to be worn on different occasions and even for different houses. At Balmoral the day-to-day black tailcoat and ordinary black-trousered livery is worn by both pages and footmen. But to tell the difference between a page (the higher-ranking) and a footman, look out for the pages' dark blue coats with velvet collars, black waistcoats and gold buttons. The footmen sport the same except that they have scarlet waistcoats. They all wear medals if they are entitled to do so.

The footmen wear state livery on state occasions – red breeches, black pumps, scarlet jacket and pink stockings. The white shirt is collarless with a lace frill. The jacket has a black rosette on the back of the collar to commemorate the death of Queen Victoria's husband, Prince Albert. It is, in fact, exactly the same livery that was in use when Prince Albert died in 1861. These jackets only come out four times a year, for two state dinners, one diplomatic reception and the opening of Parliament. They are put away spotless, and they get very little wear. A sharp-eyed guest looking beyond the brilliant colour might well spot that the gold buttons sometimes won't meet and the fit is not quite perfect. But this is hardly surprising, as generations of footmen have worn the same jackets and breeches. In the old days, when the Royal Family had more staff, kitting out the footmen was a bit of a problem. Today there is surplus livery, so it is simpler to get a better fit.

Throughout the rest of the year the livery is kept in linen bags, and all the gold buttons and gold embroidery are protected by orange tissue paper which stops it from tarnishing. Ruffs are kept in boxes along with the buckled pumps. One of the old livery porters looks after this amazing treasure trove.

Powdered hair was once the absolute rule when state livery was worn. The powder was just ordinary flour, but it wasn't easy to remove. Flour and water turn into a sticky paste, and the staff used to complain that when they finished work at two in the morning they still had to go upstairs and get rid of that lot! Also, a lot of staff who went bald were convinced that powdering was the cause. Once they had no hair to powder, they were obliged to wear a wig. Nowadays, moustaches and beards are out, and all liveried staff must be clean-shaven.

Things sometimes change, but slowly. At Balmoral, well into the late sixties, the staff still wore the battledress livery that was adopted for the war years. The basic uniform was navy blue; a footman had a red shoulder cord, the pages an embroidered gold flash, and the Palace steward a band of gold on his shoulder, all of which indicated rank. All the battle blouses had EIIR, the Queen's cipher, embroidered on the chest pocket. In the war years the pages and footmen were also given military ranks. The pages were made sergeants, the footmen corporals, and as the King's staff were mostly past call-up age, the royal 'regiment' housed some of the oldest sergeants and corporals in the world!

Up until very recently, footmen were chosen in pairs of the same height, so that they matched exactly when riding on the back of the state carriages. Today the Royal Family are not as fussy.

Liveried staff were never supposed to wear glasses, and even today they must not be worn when serving dinner. You'd think there would be awful accidents, but there never seem to be. One beautiful hot summer day the Queen and Prince Philip were lunching on the East Terrace at Windsor and the pages and footmen were wearing their white battledress livery – the livery which is worn when they are on the royal yacht. The Queen was quite astounded to be asked by one of her old pages if he could wear his sunglasses. He complained that the sunlight hitting the silver salvers and the silver cutlery, not to mention it bouncing off the crystal, was hurting his eyes. He got away with it because he was one of the old-timers, one of those who always had a word of advice for a new recruit. 'Never let them see you enjoying yourself, old boy,' he would say, and it made sense in those more formal days when staff were most definitely seen and not heard.

And yet the Royal Family are enormously tolerant with their old faithfuls. They are, to a great extent, paternalistic towards those whom they employ. And from their point of view their staff must not be unnerved by them. Those who are over-awed by royalty become inefficient and drop things. All that is required is for the staff to be unobtrusive and stay in the background.

Mistakes are made. Some years ago a footman fell in love with Princess Margaret. When he was serving at table he could not keep his eyes off her, and blushed and stumbled whenever she was near him. His eyes boring into her drove her mad, and he had to be transferred to other duties. But he was not fired. The Royal Family like to keep their staff and dislike change, and can be astonishingly forbearing with faithful retainers.

With the impatience of youth, The Duke of York is sometimes not as easy-going as his parents. Before he married, he began complaining that when he was in his bedroom in the old nursery at Buckingham Palace he could hear radios playing at night. No one would believe him. He was just beginning to think he must be going mad and imagining things, when the mystery was solved. There was a guardsman pacing up and down below in the courtyard on sentry duty – but with a transistor hidden in his bearskin. The guardsman got hell. No one, but no one, disturbs a royal's sleep. Yet the style of this anachronistic family can be curiously old-fashioned. Married women are not employed as staff at Buckingham Palace (though they can belong to the Household); and if they marry, they must leave. But then the only women on the staff are the humble housemaids, the housekeeper and her deputies, and those women called dressers who act as personal maids to their royal mistress.

The queen of the royal staff, a legend in Buckingham Palace and a power behind the throne, is Miss Margaret MacDonald, born in 1904 and affectionately called Bobo by the Royal Family. Officially she is the Queen's maid and head dresser. Privately she is a loving and loyal friend – though, steeped as she is in royal etiquette, she would never presume to describe herself in this way. She has always been exceedingly formal and correct. The Queen and the Royal Family may call her Bobo, but she is Miss MacDonald to all other Palace staff; no one would dream of calling her Bobo to her face, any more than anyone would call the Queen Lilibet – her pet name. Bobo does. She always refers to her mistress as the Queen or Her Majesty – or my little lady – in public, but privately, when they are alone together and there is no one to hear, she calls her Lilibet. She is the only person in the world, outside the immediate Royal Family, who is permitted to do this.

In the fifty-odd years that she has been at the Queen's side nobody has come within an inch of getting her job or usurping her power. Even at her great age she still guards against anyone getting too near the Queen, whom she considers very much her property. She is probably the one person who can and will say anything to the Queen that she thinks she should know. She does not approve of the *Dynasty*-type shoulders the Queen has taken to wearing recently, and said so. Her power over the other staff consists in the fact that nobody knows just how much she actually tells her mistress about what goes on behind the scenes. If the Queen wants an honest opinion about how a television performance went, or how well she delivered a speech, it will be Bobo who tells her the unvarnished truth.

She is also a remarkable living proof of the Queen's loyalty to those who serve her. In 1986 Bobo had a fall and spent some time in hospital. Everyone assumed that at her great age the Queen would now retire her. Not a bit of it. Bobo still rules the roost at Buckingham Palace, just as she always has done.

Because of all these helpers, ranging from high-ranking comptrollers and secretaries, through housekeepers, clerks and chefs down to the ordinary rank and file, the Royal Family are people who live without keys, money, credit cards or even a chequebook about their person. At one time the only thing that Prince Charles and the Duke ever carried that could spoil the perfect lines of their Savile Row suits was a small silver box which contained nothing more exciting than cloves. They carried these in case they were ever served heavily seasoned food, in the belief that chewing a clove clears the breath. The boxes were kept filled with this version of Amplex from the chef's spice-box in the kitchens.

Princess Margaret is the only one member of the immediate Royal Family with a key to her own home. The only time the Queen ever carries keys is when she is visiting her cottages around Balmoral on a Sunday. Prince Charles used to have a master key to use if he needed to come into the Palace very late or over the weekend when the building is virtually shut down. This key was not, however, handed on to the Duke and Duchess of York when they made their London base Prince Charles's old apartments overlooking the Mall. Prince Andrew used to prefer London weekends, but the Duchess of York loathes weekends in the city and was delighted when the Queen decided to give her and Andrew a country home.

They chose a site at Sunninghill Park, where the Queen and Prince Philip once had a home – they never moved in as it was burned down. There the Yorks will have a ranch-style house built. Fergie somewhat surprisingly commissioned the American firm of Parish-Hadley to provide the quintessential English country house look – having fallen in love with another house, owned by the international polo player, Henryk De Kwaitkowski, and decorated by Parish-Hadley. De Kwaitkowski is a friend of Fergie's mother, Susan Barrantes.

The Queen, who also loathes weekends in London, most certainly never needs a key to any of her homes. When she is returning to Buckingham Palace, as her car comes down the Mall, followed by a police car, the police talk to each other by radio between the car and the Palace police box. The policeman at the gate will stop the traffic, and the page and duty footman will be at the door, as if by magic, at the exact moment that her car drives up.

When the Queen goes to Windsor for the weekend, as she usually does, it is even more of a performance. She leaves on a Friday afternoon, in her fifteen-year-old Rover, from the Privy Purse Gate at the Palace for the forty-minute journey. Her orderly is already waiting on the Buckingham Palace roof, standing by the flagpole. As the Rover draws off he lowers the royal standard, and immediately the vast building dies. The lights go out and everyone who can goes too, leaving only a skeleton staff on duty.

When she leaves Windsor on Monday morning, the staff there watch for her to drive off before lowering the flag over the castle. Then one of her two pages – the one who has been on duty for the weekend – telephones his opposite number in London to say the Queen has left. And up to the roof goes the flag orderly, keeping an eye out for the Rover. As it drives through the Palace gates, up goes the standard.

Though the Duke and Duchess of York have a rented country home, Castlewood House, on the edge of Windsor Great Park, they treat Buckingham Palace as their London base. Their apartment, once occupied by Prince Charles, consists of a large study, leading into an even larger sitting room which connects with the bedroom and bathroom. Here Fergie's feminine influence shows in the pastel colour scheme chosen from Jane Churchill's elegant shop in Sloane Street. The sitting room can be, and often is used for entertaining and fourteen people can be seated in comfort. However, as there is no kitchen, only a small fridge, all the food has to come down miles of corridors from the Palace kitchens below. Fergie confesses that the absence of cooking facilities helped her to lose weight, both before and after her pregnancy.

Before his marriage, Prince Andrew had earmarked for his London home an apartment once used by the Lord Chamberlain in St James's Palace. He was anxious to move out of Prince Charles's somewhat small suite of rooms in Buckingham Palace overlooking the Mall. However, there were security problems. The front doors opened directly on to the street, and after much consideration it was decided to be too much of a risk. It was one of the rare occasions when a member of the Royal Family was not able to do exactly as he or she liked. Normally, the Royal Family never permit themselves to be inconvenienced or disturbed in any way.

For example, it is a golden rule that the Queen will not take a telephone call during dinner. No one, but no one, ever rings her until after ten. And even then only a selected few would do so – people like Lord Porchester, her racing manager, with news of the next day's racing, particularly if one of the Queen's horses was running. She might also take a call from Mrs Fenwick, who is in charge of the corgi-breeding kennels at Windsor, and might perhaps call to say that one of the bitches had had puppies. If she was in the middle of dinner, the Queen would not take a call from the Lord God Almighty. The only time that anyone at the Palace can recall the rule ever being broken was if Prince Andrew managed to get through to the Palace when he was on active duty in the Falklands War.

Another of the many royal privileges is that they are not subject to customs and immigration checks. Nor are those who travel with them: their staff could quite easily be drug smugglers, yet the royal luggage is never searched. About a week after they return home, a customs officer comes and has a chat with the travelling yeoman, the member of staff in charge of all the Queen's travelling arrangements. He then signs customs declarations, and if there is anything to declare it is done then.

The Queen is virtually above the law, but there is no way that she would ever break it. She is the one British citizen who could take her beloved corgis in and out of Britain just as she wished. But she would be breaking the strict quarantine laws that exist for everyone else in Britain, and therefore when the Queen goes abroad the corgis stay at home.

She never travels by public transport, but uses the royal yacht, the aircraft of the Queen's Flight and the royal train. It was early in 1987 that the Queen was given a new royal train, though she doesn't get the engine. A royal train consists of a series of special carriages which are linked to an ordinary British Rail engine. These are the second set of new carriages of her reign. The first ones were very antiquated, and she was heard to complain that they had square wheels. Of course the royal carriages are a considerable improvement on those that the public use. The Queen and Prince Charles have a proper bathroom, Prince Philip a shower.

Prince Charles took great interest in the furnishing of the new royal train. The two coaches that are for his own use are decorated in natural wood with easy chairs upholstered in dark blue flowered chinz. The paintings are from the Prince's personal collection, as is the lavatory seat – a magnificent mahogany throne which is reputed to have cost more than £1000. But apart from these little personal touches the new carriages are actually rather dull, with none of the glamour of the older royal trains. This is all part of the family's anxiety not to appear ostentatious in a country where unemployment is rife. There even used to be a royal staff train, but now they travel by ordinary second-class sleeper when they are going up to Balmoral for the summer.

Food on the royal train is provided by the same Inter-City catering services as on any other British passenger train, but undoubtedly they try harder. The menus are agreed beforehand with the travelling yeoman, and both Prince Charles and Prince Philip frequently hold working lunches and dinners on board. Surprisingly, the dining saloon can comfortably accommodate twelve people.

Sometimes the Queen decides not to bring out the entire train for a journey. If she is going somewhere alone, it is more likely that she will have a couple of special carriages put on the back of an ordinary Inter-City train, particularly if she is just going to pick up the royal yacht at Southampton before setting off on the Western Isle cruise that the family take every summer.

The Queen Mother never takes public transport, either; planes and helicopters are her favourite methods of travelling. The rest of the Royal Family, however, might well take a first-class seat on an ordinary scheduled flight, or book a complete railway compartment – that's if they can't hitch a lift on either the yacht or one of the royal aircraft. Prince Charles finds trains very relaxing and would like to travel by them more than he does. Princess Diana usually flies. The family fly people back and forth to Balmoral when they are there in the summer. Charles Martyn, the Queen's hairdresser, flies up for one visit through the holiday, and then comes back by train. The Queen, ever thoughtful, sees that he has a small picnic hamper specially prepared by the chef, as the overnight train from Aberdeen has no restaurant car abroad.

That same thoughtfulness is evident in her annual party for handicapped people. It is exactly the same as a Buckingham Palace garden party. The guests arrive in ambulances from ex-servicemen's and servicewomen's homes, such as the Star and Garter, and they include the famous Chelsea Pensioners. Because most of those invited cannot wander about the Palace grounds, the Queen provides entertainment, asking stars like Vera Lynn, the singer who was the forces' wartime favourite, to come and sing. It's not the easiest party to organize, as men and women from the St John's Ambulance Brigade have to wheel all the guests from the Bow Room, down the steps and across the lawn to the tea tents. The Queen herself always goes to this party if she is in England, but if not there are always other members of the Royal Family there.

The Queen must entertain more people of every class, nationality and rank than any other living person – including the President of the United States, whom she has entertained and been entertained by in return. The Queen hosted a party for the President and his lady on the royal yacht on her trip to the United States in 1983. The enormous yacht, with its crew of 270 who keep her spotless and gleaming, is royal style at the height of grandeur. The dining room where the Reagans ate seats sixty guests, and they would have eaten off porcelain plates which were once used by Edward VII. The *Britannia* has its own fine crystal and silver, and the table is always decorated with gold, scale-model galleons and racing yachts.

The Reagans would have been treated to the Queen's unique way of rounding off a dinner party aboard the *Britannia*. After liqueurs, coffee and conversation on board, she escorts her magnificently attired guests on to the royal deck where below, on the jetty, are the band of the Royal Marines. The string section will have already played all through dinner, but now the more robust brass and drum section takes over. They beat the retreat, marching up and down, playing English military marches. The Marine officer then salutes his monarch and her distinguished guests, and off they go. The evening is over.

2

BREAKFAST WITH THE ROYALS

Breakfast at any one of the royal households is treated with the respect that this first meal of the day is due. The Queen likes to eat in an air of cathedral calm; the early morning is for her the most relaxing time of the day.

Just before nine the Queen's footman hovers in the royal kitchen waiting for the phone call from Her Majesty's page, who has also been hovering but just outside her sitting room. When he hears Her Majesty coming through from her dressing room, he immediately goes to the internal telephone system to summon the royal breakfast. Minutes later, after travelling a few hundred yards, the food is carried on a large silver tray into the Queen's private dining room.

The Queen eats breakfast in the company of her husband, Prince Philip, when he is not away on an engagement, though she enjoys a much heartier meal than he is prepared to tackle. Both the Queen and the Duke drink coffee – a special blend of their own which comes from the Palace coffee room, whose other duty is to make the breakfast toast. The coffee is freshly ground and served in simple brown earthenware pots which pour from the side. Making this royal brew is a very slow process because the coffee room ladies use the drip system; boiling water never touches a grain of their special blend, for the Royal Family believe that it ruins coffee. Yet, conversely, the milk served with it is always boiling – the Queen and the Duke drink white coffee at breakfast. The coffee room seem to have got it right, however, as those fortunate enough to have taken coffee at the Palace say it is truly delicious.

The Duke's breakfast-eating habits have changed over the years. There was a time when he had his own electric frying pan which he kept in the page's waiting room so that he could rustle himself up some early morning bacon and eggs. The Palace is so huge that very often food arrives at its destination cold, and the frying pan was the Duke's answer to the problem. Today, like his eldest son, he has turned to a health food diet, and his breakfast is more likely to consist of bran flakes, natural yoghurt and honey. The electric frying pan has been relegated to the kitchen.

When at Buckingham Palace, the Queen and the Duke usually eat in her little private dining room which leads off her sitting room. The table is always formally set, with fresh fruit and flowers from the royal gardens placed on brilliantly white linen. There is an electric hotplate on the sideboard to keep the dish of the day warm.

The Queen never breakfasts in bed, not even when she is on holiday. She considers it a lazy habit, though she does encourage her guests to take their breakfast in their rooms. It gives everyone a little breathing space and time for privacy in the morning. The Queen Mother, on the other hand, almost always breakfasts in bed. In fact, she does not come through from her bedroom and dressing room until around eleven. Like most of us, she enjoys dozing and pottering about.

It is rare for anyone to see the Queen at breakfast time. When she stays at other people's houses she always has a tray brought to her room, but even then she doesn't sit and eat breakfast in bed. Her Majesty is not one to lie in bed. In fact, it always amazes those closest to her that she only ever allows herself that weakness when she gets a cold. Then she goes straight to bed in order to be well again as soon as possible. When the Queen is ill and can't keep her appointments, it makes for a great many disappointed people. If any of the family get anything infectious they are never visited by their nearest and dearest, for the same reason.

The Queen always has a hearty, traditional British cooked meal in the morning – porridge, followed by bacon and eggs or occasionally the special favourite, a kipper. A solid breakfast to start the day is a habit from her childhood, and the tradition continues. When the Queen's grandchildren come to stay with her, they are always served a hot meal at eight-thirty. Scrambled eggs are a favourite, but this dish is rarely served to adults for breakfast. Once the Royal Family grow up they prefer their scrambled eggs served with smoked salmon as a light before-the-theatre dish. In the same way, though sausages

– Harrods best – are always on offer for breakfast for guests, the Royal Family regard them as a barbecue dish.

The Queen likes to have every one of the national dailies at hand, arranged on a small card table beside her while she eats. The Duke, like many other husbands, grunts from behind the *Financial Times*. While they read the papers, they also have the radio playing softly. Every morning she herself brings the radio through from her bedroom and sets it in a corner, tuned to the talking station, Radio 4.

At the same time her pipe major is piping away below in the courtyard outside the dining room window. He plays Scottish airs for twenty minutes every morning, except Sundays – a tradition that goes back to Queen Victoria's day. This is a morning ritual which is so much part of the Queen's day that her pipe major only takes holidays when she is on overseas tours.

If the Queen has been away on a state visit and feels she has put on weight from too many banquets, she will start her breakfast with half a grapefruit. The pastry chef cuts it so each segment can be lifted out with a spoon; he takes out all the pips, and then puts a ring of greaseproof paper on top to stop the fruit from drying out. When the fruit is served, accompanied by a special silver spoon with which to eat it, a page carefully removes the paper. The Queen believes implicitly in the slimming powers of a grapefruit, and eating half of one for breakfast is about all she ever does in the way of dieting.

Across the park at Kensington Palace, Prince Charles and Princess Diana eat very little breakfast and, because of their different heavy schedules, they may not necessarily eat together. Princess Diana, like the Queen, goes for grapefruit – pink grapefruit, followed by muesli, brown toast and weak coffee. It is her second cup of the morning. The butler, Harold Brown, has already discreetly woken her by a gentle tap on the door, and then appeared with a silver tray holding the wake-up coffee and freshly squeezed orange juice. The Prince doesn't like coffee and never has. But since his marriage he has taken to drinking the rather exotic lapsang souchong tea, followed by bran flakes, wholemeal toast and his favourite honey.

Breakfast with the Waleses is very much a movable feast. Some mornings the Princess gets up, puts on a tracksuit and takes herself off in her Ford Escort for a ten-minute drive to Buckingham Palace to have a swim in the Palace pool. Other mornings, she takes the opportunity to lie in.

The Prince is an early riser. He listens to the BBC farming programme on Radio 4. He has his morning bath, drawn by his valet, Ken Stronach, who also lays out his clothes in the Prince's dressing room. Then the valet discreetly disappears while his master dresses.

Both the Prince and Princess have the same arrangement of bathroom and dressing room each side of their bedroom, so that they bathe and dress in privacy. They do sleep in a double bed – a huge four-poster which was about the only item of his personal furniture that Charles brought with him from Buckingham Palace.

When the Waleses go to their country home, Highgrove, they usually try to take their first meal of the day in the nursery with Princes William and Harry. Indeed, given the opportunity, they like to take all their meals with the two little princes. This is something new and modern in royal life, as the Queen never breakfasted with any of her children when they were small.

But then the Prince of Wales has always enjoyed the nursery atmosphere at breakfast time. When his brothers Prince Edward and Andrew were little, Nanny Anderson, who brought up all four of the Queen's children, was in charge of the nursery. Prince Charles would appear most mornings at eight-thirty to have breakfast with his brothers and also to see Mabel Anderson, who was one of his favourite people. It was a great disappointment to him that Princess Diana insisted on having a younger, less traditional nanny when Prince William came along. Perhaps, by starting each day eating breakfast with young William and Harry, he is continuing the habit of his youth as well as ensuring that he is never remote from his children. He also still rather likes nursery food. For many years he always had a glass of milk for breakfast. Now he considers it too high in fat and cholesterol, and prefers his tea.

If it seems odd that Princess Diana and Prince Charles do not breakfast together in London, one has to remember that even when the Royal Family are all gathered together at the Queen's holiday home, Balmoral, or her weekend home, the vast and rambling Windsor Castle, they rarely take breakfast together. Guests visiting the Royal Family are treated – well, like royalty. Yet even so, at Balmoral and Windsor they will rarely see the Queen before lunch. The exception to this rule is when the court is at Sandringham. Every year the Royal Family, their household and staff spend a six-week holiday here that starts immediately after Christmas. The emphasis of these weeks is on pheasant shooting, and there is a constant house party of friends and influential people who are invited for the sport.

At Sandringham, as at the other royal homes, what they call the morning kitchen is divided. There is the coffee room, which is like an old-fashioned still room and deals with continental-type breakfasts and cereals and toasts. Then there is the kitchen itself, which provides cooked breakfasts. It is not a convenient arrangement for the staff: the footmen and pages (usually four of them) have to run between the two to keep the whole thing going.

The Queen and her lady guests all come down to the dining room for breakfast at Sandringham. The enormous selection of breakfast dishes is laid out on the sideboard that runs the length of the room. There is always one main egg dish, accompanied by bacon, plus something fishy – maybe haddock or cod. Occasionally a kedgeree is served, but only when there is some left-over salmon. The Queen's favourite kippers are usually on offer. For those who do not like hot food, there is always a huge York ham on a silver dish with a page waiting to carve. Some guests with large appetites manage both hot and cold. Porridge is served with big jugs of farm cream, but it is rarely eaten because it is so damaging to the waistline!

One of the royals' most delicious, if dreadfully fattening, breakfast dishes is an invention of a long-ago Palace chef and it has no name. It is made from a thick slice of bread with some of the crumb scooped out to leave an egg-shaped space. The remaining bread slice is deep fried until crisp and golden, and then a perfectly poached egg is dropped into the centre opening.

When on holiday, if the Duke has shot a snipe the day before he'll eat it on toast for breakfast. Snipe are tiny little things, difficult to bring down because they weave in flight. Prince Charles would never shoot them; he felt sorry for them.

Breakfast is served from eight-thirty. On Sundays it is served half an hour later so that everyone, including the Queen, gets a bit longer in bed. The meal is always set up the previous night. Immediately after dinner, when the candelabra have been cleared to the silver pantry, the two duty footmen put heat mats and a thick baize cover on the superbly polished sideboard and long dining table. Then everything is covered with a white linen tablecloth before setting plates and cruets. The only time the Royal Family ever use linen is at breakfast and tea. The spectacular white damask tablecloths and enormous napkins used in the morning belonged to Queen Victoria, and they are still going strong.

It seems incredible that this wonderful embossed linen can have lasted for more than eighty years, but then one has to remember that it is brought out for only six weeks of the year. The Balmoral linen, also once the property of Queen Victoria, is used for only ten weeks in the summer. So the table linen lasts much longer than in an ordinary household. Also, it is not beaten about in modern laundries, but washed by the staff, whereas the marvellous old linen in London and Windsor goes to a special little laundry in Clapham. Once a week a black and gold van from the Sycamore Laundry arrives to pick up the week's washing in great old-fashioned wicker laundry baskets. Every item is returned neatly folded between layers of tissue paper. Incidentally, napkin rings are considered very unstylish and are now quite unknown on royal tables, though they were used for the duration of the war to save on the laundry bills. Today the linen is only ever used once before being laundered.

The breakfast china is simple, yet still goes back several generations. Present-day royals nearly always eat off china which is stamped with an ancestor's cipher. The cutlery is plain silver – gilt cutlery is not used at breakfast time. Neither are fish knives and forks. The Royal Family never use them, considering them passé and really rather vulgar. The table is functional, set for convenience rather than formality. At each place the footman lays a cereal spoon and two sets of knives and forks, one for hot food and one for cold. Fruit plates are run down the centre of the table, with a fruit knife and fork on each plate.

Butter is made into little pats in the coffee room by pressing it between two old-fashioned wooden moulds. Some of these imprint a motif, such as a thistle, into the butter, which, of course, is also just at the right temperature to spread easily. The Royal Family do not like very warm rooms, so though butter is never put in the fridge it doesn't melt too easily. If anyone feels chilly, the Queen suggests they put on another sweater.

There are no finger bowls and no flowers on the table. Nor are there any special seating arrangements for breakfast – people settle where they land. The Queen has the only 'reserved' seat, usually centre of the table, with her back to the window. There are no visible signs to show where she sits, but her guests are 'regulars' and know the rules.

The fruit from last night's dinner will have been rearranged in big silver dishes. Cooper's jams – the brand the Royal Family always use – have been emptied into crystal bowls, and honey is served in pots with china bees on the lids. The Royal Family love honey. They collect it from anywhere. When anyone gives either Prince Philip or Prince Charles some local honey they are both genuinely thrilled. And they always buy it for themselves at the Scottish sales of work which they like to patronize.

The shoot begins at exactly nine-thirty every morning except Sunday, when, so as not to offend anybody, there is no shooting. The men – and it is only the men who shoot in the morning – are expected to be ready and on time. The greatest crime in royal eyes is unpunctuality, and the Duke of Edinburgh can become very impatient indeed if he is kept waiting.

In this he takes after the Queen's grandfather, King George V, who actually put all the clocks at Sandringham forward by one hour so that the royal shooting parties would have more daylight to kill more pheasants. The first thing Edward VIII (later the Duke of Windsor) did when he became King was to put the clocks right. He loved shooting, but he needed to make a gesture of his own independence against his father's draconian rule. Royalty can be cavalier with clocks even today. One New Year's Eve at Sandringham, the Queen Mother decided to have New Year early – and had the staff put all the clocks forward by one hour!

Breakfast is served three-quarters of an hour before the shoot begins and the clever ones get in quickly. The Duke will be at the front door at nine-thirty ready to go, Land Rovers with their engines running standing outside. Those who may have stayed up too late listening to Princess Margaret playing and singing at the piano have been known to grab a bap (a soft Scottish bread roll), push a piece of ham into it and eat on the run.

Immediately the guns have gone out, the Queen goes upstairs to her private room. Her lady-in-waiting takes care of any mail that has arrived, and the lady guests are expected to amuse themselves for half an hour. Some may go for a walk, others might read the papers. Princess Diana usually gets on with her needlepoint in this 'free time'.

The reason that the Queen comes down for breakfast at Sandringham and nowhere else is because Sandringham was the subject of an attempt at royal reform in the early seventies. The Duke had decided that life on this royal estate, which is the Queen's own personal property, was to be streamlined; fewer servants would be employed, everyone would serve themselves with food, and even the guests would 'muck in' so as to cut down on the running costs. 'Mucking in' is a favourite royal expression, and one that strikes terror into the Palace staff. They know from experience that 'mucking in' generally just means a great deal more work for them.

The changes were short-lived. Not a lot of 'mucking in' went on, but some of Prince Philip's plans did work. In the old days the senior staff and officials were served all their meals by junior staff, just as in a Victorian household. That has finished. Staff serve themselves – with the exception of the eighty-four-year-old Bobo MacDonald. When told that in future she would no longer have her meals brought to her room, Bobo developed a very bad cold and could not possibly leave her room. The cold lingered, and lingered, and lingered. Bobo is still the only member of staff who is served her tray, in her room, just like in the old days.

The only other surviving reform was that breakfast is now self-service for the dozen or so guests who are invited at any one time to Sandringham. But there are footmen standing behind the hot plates ready and waiting to lift off the lids, so it's not too arduous or primitive. And the footmen do put the food on to the guest's plate. No one is greedy, because the Queen is irritated if she sees uneaten food left on plates going back to the kitchen. She doesn't mind how much people eat, but she loathes waste.

And at Sandringham, always present at breakfast, clustered around their mistress, are the Queen's corgis. It's just unfortunate if any guest does not like dogs or has strong views about their presence at mealtimes. Where the Queen goes, her corgis go, the patter of paws making a splendid early warning system that the Queen is nearby.

The routine is different at both Windsor and Balmoral. At Windsor, guests always breakfast in their room, having given their breakfast order to the page in charge the night before. They are asked to choose between a cooked or a coffee room breakfast, which is usually just toast and fruit. The cooked breakfast comes on big silver trays on superb silver dishes with boiling water set underneath – a necessary precaution, as at Windsor it is not an exaggeration to say that the kitchen can be nearly a mile from some of the rooms. Indeed, the former Prime Minister Edward Heath was unwise enough to order boiled eggs for breakfast when he was a guest at the Castle. They arrived bullet-hard. He sent them back, and tried again. The second lot were equally hard. It is not possible to serve soft-boiled eggs in the bedrooms of Windsor Castle.

At Balmoral, where again everything revolves around sport, the gentlemen come downstairs for breakfast in tweed plus-fours or their kilts, and the ladies are encouraged to remain in their rooms. The Duke of Edinburgh takes his breakfast with the Queen in her private sitting room. Without the royal presence, breakfast is more relaxed for guests than at Sandringham, but the royal standards are still maintained.

Even though the Balmoral holiday takes place between August and October, Scotland can be freezing cold, and so the Queen provides her breakfasting guests with an electric fire, one that just plugs into the wall. And if it gets very cold there might be a second fire in the corner of the room. Log fires are reserved for the drawing room.

A British breakfast would not be complete without the newspapers, and the royal newsagent's bill is a high one. They would never dream of watching morning television and like to make sure all guests have a paper to read over breakfast. A couple of full sets are laid out in the dining room for the men. Each lady guest is delivered a paper (not of her choice but what is available) with her breakfast tray. Sabrina Guinness, once a girlfriend of Prince Charles, had her Balmoral weekend ruined when the morning paper delivered to her room featured exaggerated details of their romance. She suspected that the staff could not resist it. The Queen and the Queen Mother always have a full set of papers of their own. After breakfast the footmen gather up all the papers and place them in the drawing room. Actually at remote Balmoral the papers arrive so late that they often become afternoon reading.

Those who breakfast downstairs have a huge choice of food decided by the chef, ranging from sausages or kidneys to coffee and croissants. Yet no guest of Her Majesty can expect elaborate meals. All the Royal Family have simple tastes. For example, on Easter Sunday simple boiled eggs are always served, as this is an occasion on which no one but the Queen's immediate family will be present. The chef is forever suggesting something more exciting in the menu book, but the Queen firmly crosses out his choice and writes 'boiled eggs' instead.

The meal is eaten in the Queen's private dining room at Windsor. It is also one of the rare occasions when the royal grandchildren – Princess Diana's William and Harry, and Princess Anne's Zara and Peter – sit down with the family. Prince Philip always presides over a table decorated with fluffy Easter chicks and little silver paper-wrapped chocolate Easter eggs. Small gifts are also exchanged (see p. 158).

Undoubtedly the reason why the Queen insists on plain boiled eggs for Easter breakfast is because this is the tradition in Britain. Normally a royal breakfast is a much more elaborate affair. The mushrooms and tomatoes served will be home grown on the Queen's estates, and at Balmoral she also has free-range eggs from one of the farms on the estate. These are gathered for the consumption of the Queen, her family and her guests. The staff get ordinary eggs, bought in bulk.

Prince Charles and Princess Diana have now become so diet-conscious that eating is no longer a great pleasure to either of them.

Yet there was a time when he rather enjoyed his breakfasts, and he still does when travelling on the royal train. British Rail have always had a reputation for cooking delicious English breakfasts, and the royal train is staffed by ordinary British Rail staff. Both the Prince and his father marvel at how the railway chefs produce a splendid, piping hot meal in a tiny railway carriage. All too often, in their view, the royal chefs, with acres of space down in the basement of Buckingham Palace and every imaginable piece of equipment, still don't get it right.

Prince Charles and Prince Philip are quite likely to forget their new health food principles when they are on the royal train. The train usually stops at a siding overnight, and they like to get up in time to eat before the train moves on, so as not to impair their digestion with a lot of rocking about. The Queen and Prince Philip use British Rail's best crockery and ordinary knives and forks. Prince Charles provides his own. He also keeps a bike on the train and often goes for an early morning ride, or a jog, before breakfast. He's been known to startle railwaymen on their way to work who weren't expecting to run into the Prince of Wales. And the water from his Badedas bath can be seen swirling away on the siding.

Normally, when any member of the Royal Family is travelling and staying in hotels, he or she becomes dependent on room service. And that is the reason why the Queen prefers to take the royal yacht or an aircraft of the Queen's Flight. On the yacht and in her own plane she is at home and can control what she eats. For royalty, the trouble with staying in hotels is that they are swamped with food and appalled by the amount served, particularly at breakfast time.

Royalty travel with quite a lot of their own food. They take their own cereal – Prince Charles likes Kellogg's bran flakes – honey and lemon drink, and for tea chocolate Bath Oliver biscuits, which require very strong teeth. Their honey is never left behind at the hotel, but packed and taken back to the Palace.

A typical range of royal breakfast dishes at one of their principal homes would be:

Cereals (packet)	Porridge	Toast/croissants
Fresh orange juice	Grapefruit	Fresh fruit
Boiled eggs	Bacon	Mushrooms
Scrambled eggs	Kidneys	Grilled tomatoes
Fried eggs	Sausages	Sauté potatoes
Poached eggs	Smoked haddock	Cold game
Omelettes	Kedgeree	Kippers
Cooper's jams	Honey	Cooper's marmalade

All the recipes below serve four people unless otherwise stated.

KEDGEREE

Kedgeree is popular because of the large number of salmon that the royals catch in the River Dee in Scotland. It can, of course, also be made with smoked haddock, cod, turbot or halibut.

1 lb (450 g) long-grain rice
3 eggs
12 oz (350 g) cooked fish
2 oz (60 g) butter
¼ pint (150 ml) single cream
A little milk
Salt and pepper to taste

Put the rice into a large saucepan with 3 pints (1.75 litres) of boiling salted water. Boil until tender – roughly 20 minutes. Meanwhile, hard-boil the eggs for 8 minutes and then plunge them into cold water. Drain the cooked rice and rinse it in cold water. Flake the fish, removing all skin and bones. Chop the eggs coarsely. Put a saucepan on a low heat with the butter, add the rice, then the eggs (reserve a few bits for decoration), followed by the fish, and fold everything together well with a wooden spoon. Add the cream and milk and seasoning to taste. Decorate with the reserved chopped hard-boiled egg and serve hot or cold.

POACHED SMOKED HADDOCK

For each person:
1 smoked haddock fillet
Milk and water for cooking
Large knob of butter
1 poached egg (optional)

Wash the haddock, place it in a shallow pan and just cover with a mixture of milk and water. Bring to the boil, turn down the heat and poach gently until the flesh just begins to flake. Serve immediately, with a large knob of cold butter and, if liked, a poached egg on top.

BACON OMELETTE

Of all egg dishes Prince Philip prefers omelettes, and often insists on cooking them himself in his own glass-topped frying pan which he plugs into a power point in the dining room.

For each person:
2 large fresh eggs
1 tablespoon water
Salt and pepper to taste
1 oz (25 g) butter
2 rashers streaky bacon, rinds removed, crisply fried or grilled
Parsley for garnish

Beat the eggs well to break up the yolks, and season to taste. Add the water. In an 8-inch (20-cm) non-stick omelette pan melt the butter until frothy, swirling it around the base to cover the pan completely. Cook for about a minute over a high heat until the bottom is set, then loosen the edges with a spatula. Lift the edges and tip pan so that any runny mixture flows underneath. When the omelette is set, fold it in half and slide it on to a warm plate. Serve with the bacon, garnished with parsley.

SCRAMBLED EGGS

This favourite royal breakfast dish is also often eaten as a late-night supper snack. After the wedding of Prince Andrew and Sarah Ferguson, the Queen and Prince Philip joined other royals at Claridge's for a private supper party in the evening. There they all ate scrambled eggs while watching the wedding on television.

For each person:
Knob of butter
2 large fresh eggs
1 tablespoon creamy milk or single cream
Salt and pepper
Buttered toast to serve

Heat the butter until melted in a non-stick saucepan. Beat the eggs with the milk or cream and seasoning. Pour the mixture into the pan and cook for a few minutes over a medium heat, stirring constantly, until the bottom of the mixture begins to thicken slightly. Reduce the heat and continue cooking and stirring until the eggs are set according to taste. Serve on or with freshly made buttered toast.

BREAKFAST KIDNEYS

For each person:
2 lamb's kidneys
Knob of butter
1 slice day-old bread

Skin the kidneys if necessary, and cut them in two lengthwise. Heat the butter in a frying pan until it begins to sizzle, then sauté the kidneys briskly. When they are no longer pink in the middle, transfer them to a heated dish and keep warm. Serve with croûtons made from bread cut into 1-inch (2-cm) squares and fried in the remaining butter – add a little more if required. When golden brown, transfer the croûtons to the serving dish with the kidneys.

PORRIDGE

For 2 large or 4 small servings:
2 oz (60 g) medium oatmeal
1 pint (600 ml) water
1 teaspoon salt
Milk or cream, and runny honey or golden syrup, to serve

Bring the water and salt to the boil. Slowly sprinkle in the oatmeal. Keep the water on the boil and stir constantly to prevent sticking. Simmer gently until the porridge begins to swell, then reduce the heat and half cover the pan for 30 minutes, stirring at intervals. When the porridge is thick and creamy, taste and add more salt if required. Turn off the heat and let the porridge rest for 5 minutes. More boiling water can be added if the porridge becomes too thick. Serve with cold milk or cream and dribble on honey or golden syrup.

3

ROYAL HOUSE GUEST

The Queen likes to entertain, and indeed does a great deal of it. But her style is not to invite a few friends in for dinner or for drinks. Some other members of the Royal Family entertain with 'one-off' dinner and cocktail parties, but when the Queen's friends are invited it is almost always for a long weekend.

She rarely entertains personal friends at Buckingham Palace – only heads of state, dignitaries or visiting royalty. Buckingham Palace is, to her, no more than an office in which she is forced to live for four nights a week. A dinner party or a banquet at Buckingham Palace is rather like the head of a vast corporation entertaining in the board room. Therefore, when the Queen has guests they are invited to her private homes – Balmoral and Sandringham, or her favourite official residence, Windsor Castle. Even at Windsor personal friends are only entertained for an occasional Sunday lunch, but this ancient castle is the setting when she gives a house party for Royal Ascot week in June.

The Windsor Sunday lunches do have one extra purpose – this is the time when the Queen's children invite their friends to meet their distinguished parents. They have sought permission well in advance, of course – no one drops in on the Queen!

Most of the other entertaining at this, the largest inhabited castle in the world, is called Dine and Sleep. People whom protocol demands to be invited come for dinner are given a bed for the night and breakfast in the morning, and then sent politely on their way.

To be a personal guest of the Queen is quite a different matter. And in the two royal holiday breaks of January and August the Queen constantly entertains. She usually invites about four to six couples at one time, including the latest girlfriends and boyfriends of the younger members of the family. Everyone arrives on the Thursday and leaves after lunch on the Sunday.

The venue in January is Sandringham House in Norfolk for the pheasant shooting, and in August Balmoral Castle for the grouse. Invitations are sent out at least six weeks before the great day, but mostly, it must be said, they are posted to what the Palace staff call the 'Queen's regulars'. These are her friends who are generally asked at exactly the same time each year. The routine is so consistent that they hardly need the invitation at all. The Queen and her family hate change and basically like a quiet life with no great fuss, so they find it more comfortable if they are with people who are not over-awed by them.

It would be social death, of course, for a 'regular' if the invitation did not arrive one year. It can happen, but usually only to those who divorce or find themselves in some other kind of public trouble. Until the scandal dies down the Queen will usually leave these unfortunates off her public visiting list. However, she is very loyal to her friends and will probably continue to see them quietly. What she cannot countenance, as the head of the established Church, is entertaining couples who live together but who are not married. In the changing world of the eighties this can be something of a problem.

The atmosphere at both the Queen's private homes is very relaxed. There are no dos and don'ts as most of their guests know how to behave, and are *au fait* with the rules of mixing with royalty. Of course, none of the Queen's friends, however close, would dream of calling her by her first name. Though they may have known her since childhood, they still curtsey when she comes into the room or if they meet her in a corridor; they still never leave a room until she does, and still never sit before she is seated.

Most of the Queen's friends have stately homes of their own and are wealthy people, but even for the rich to stay with her is a treat. These days all the money in the world cannot normally buy the superb staff and the standard of service which royalty enjoy.

The Queen's visitors are not, as you might expect, provided with transport. They get themselves to the nearest railway station, unless they decide to drive. Most people do drive to Sandringham, which is only 110 miles from London, but those invited to Balmoral are more likely to go by train or plane to far-flung (by British standards)

Aberdeen, the nearest large town to the Queen's Scottish home. The Queen sends a minibus to meet them and drive them the sixty miles to Balmoral Castle. At one time Rolls-Royces were sent, but the minibus is one of the royal economies that have been put into operation over the years.

The invitation suggests in an informal way that guests should arrive around six in time for drinks. And when they leave the minibus outside the double front doors, guests are guided to the salon by the Queen's equerry or lady-in-waiting. Very close friends may well be met at the door by the Queen herself. Meanwhile the luggage is being taken round to the back door by the luggage man who, oddly, is still called the coal man. The coal men's jobs vanished once central heating was installed, and their new role is to handle all luggage.

Balmoral has 120 staff to look after the family, the Queen's senior staff and her guests; Sandringham has rather fewer. Lady guests are looked after by housemaids who wear short black dresses, not unlike those of a saucy French maid. Gentlemen are in the care of footmen resplendent in tailcoated livery. The Queen personally inspects the rooms before her guests arrive, making sure they are properly appointed. She checks that there is Malvern water at hand, soap in the bathroom and newly published books for bedtime reading. She is sent so many books by publishers that there are plenty to put around. She herself shows guests to their quarters at about seven o'clock, fussing like any hostess to make sure that they have all they need. She then leaves, giving them time to prepare themselves for dinner.

Once in their rooms guests find a little guide on the dressing table which will have been left by either the sergeant footman or the housekeeper. On it will be typed the guests' own names together with the name of the maid and the footman who will be looking after them. There is a note on the back of the card which advises about tipping, suggesting that £5 is about the right amount. The royals do not want to create inflation, but neither do they want their staff to be under-tipped. Very close friends don't get these instructions, as they know the form. Footmen and maids might look after several people and often finish up with anything between £10 and £20 extra a week.

Guests only tip these two categories of staff, which causes some jealousy among the chauffeurs and chefs.

By the time the guests are in their rooms, the maid will already have unpacked the luggage and put everything away. She will also have guessed – and the Queen's maids rarely get it wrong – exactly what the lady will be wearing for dinner that night, and taken the dress and the man's evening clothes away to be pressed.

There will be fresh flowers in the room, fresh fruit and a small dish of Bendick's mints, which are very much sought after by the staff. The popular guest is the one who doesn't eat them, leaving yet another little treat for the footmen and the maids. Each room at Windsor, as at the Palace, is furnished with a small drinks tray on which sit three tiny decanters containing gin, scotch and sherry. These hold just about three measures each. Wine is never served in the bedrooms, and only semi-official guests get the decanters. For close friends in the private homes there is no alcohol of any kind in the room. People have been known to bring hip flasks!

Once the guests have changed for dinner, the maid asks what her lady requires for breakfast, since here it is only the men who breakfast downstairs. Orders are always taken the night before to give the kitchen plenty of time to prepare.

Everyone gets their own bedroom and sitting room, but surprisingly not all have a bathroom en suite. The rooms that do have a private bath and lavatory go to the most important guests, and unlike other households, the most important are the Royal Family themselves. Members of the family are always given the best accommodation. There is one exception – the Prime Minister. It is a tradition that he or she is always invited for one weekend at Balmoral – usually the first weekend in September. The suite the Prime Minister occupies has pictures of all past premiers on the walls, hung on cream wallpaper which, like most things in the Queen's private homes, dates back to Great-great-grandma, Queen Victoria. And they still have masses and masses of spare rolls to replace any wear and tear.

Other guests may have to double up on the washing facilities, and one guest, the wife of Commander Michael Parker, ex-equerry to Prince Philip, tells the story of a morning encounter with Prince

Philip in the corridor – she in her dressing gown, and he in a shortie towelling robe. Feeling extremely silly, she immediately dropped into a deep curtsey to find herself staring at a pair of very hairy knees.

Even when the rooms do have their own baths, the plumbing leaves much to be desired at both houses. The pipes at Balmoral are ancient. They gurgle throughout the night and they also relay sound, so that in some rooms conversations from another part of the house are quite clearly heard.

Dinner is at eight-fifteen, and a quarter of an hour later when the Queen Mother is in the house to allow for her notorious unpunctuality. First-timer guests are always escorted to the drawing room. It is quite easy to get lost, and the Queen would not wish her guests to be embarrassed by being late. All the regulars know the way. And when the younger members of the family bring boyfriends and girlfriends to stay (having been declared persona grata after a Windsor Sunday lunch), their hosts always collect them and guide them to the drawing room. In his bachelor days many likely ladies were taken down to dinner by Prince Charles. The Duchess of York, like Princess Diana, got to know the Royal Family here, and no doubt the girl whom Prince Edward marries will first be a weekend guest at one of the private homes.

The dining room at Balmoral is very grand, with silver figures depicting Scottish sports – tossing the caber, putting the shot – decorating the table. The Royal Family always dress for dinner when they have guests. It may be sweaters and pearls and sensible shoes for the daytime, but the ladies are expected to pull out all the stops in the evening. The men, of course, sport a dinner jacket, or, if in Scotland and they are entitled to wear one, the kilt. The Queen takes all her best jewellery to Balmoral with her, and wears it, so guests rustle up the grandest they have, too. The Queen always enters the dining room last at Buckingham Palace and Windsor Castle, the official residences. Everyone else is expected to be in position, standing behind their chairs, before she appears. At her own homes she herself leads the guests in from pre-dinner drinks in the drawing room. The page announces that dinner is served immediately the first course is outside, ready to go on the table.

The Queen has already prepared what the royals call a dinner board. We would call it a table plan, and she settles down to organize this once she has had tea. The seats are rotated for every night of a guest's stay, so that everyone gets a chance to sit next to a royal. Working this out can be quite a complicated task, but it is one that the Queen prefers to do herself. The completed plan is left by the drinks tray, from which people help themselves, so that everyone can check where they are sitting.

Guests follow Her Majesty into the dining room quite informally. There's no 'piping in' by the pipe major as there was even in the days when the Queen Mother shared thc throne. But at Balmoral the piper still does walk round the table playing after the coffee has been served. (The Queen Mother always drinks tea.) The ladies still retire, leaving the gentlemen to their cigars and port for about thirty minutes, before the entire party congregates in the drawing room for after-dinner drinks.

At this point, the guests can either steel themselves to play parlour games – charades is a great favourite – or a new film might be shown. The Royal Family never switch on TV when guests are present. They enjoy watching it themselves, so the programmes they want to see are video-ed by a footman and shown in the afternoons when it's their 'free time' as well as everyone else's.

Nobody goes to bed before the Queen, and she generally says goodnight at about eleven-thirty. She still has work to do, going through the contents of her red boxes which contain state papers. This is the time for visitors to escape as well if they are ready for bed. Otherwise it is the point of the evening when Princess Margaret begins to sing and play the piano. Once the Queen has left, nobody departs from the room before Princess Margaret, and since she is the night owl of the family it can be very late before she decides to go to bed.

Guests do have to sing for their supper in small ways. At Balmoral, the Queen always gives two ghillies' (gamekeepers') balls which all the staff, the Royal Family and guests attend. These are the highlight of the annual visit for the estate workers. The women bring out their long dresses; their men wear the kilt. The Queen and the Queen Mother wear tiaras and the Royal Stuart tartan sash over their evening dresses. Guests, like the Royal Family, are expected to dance with as many of the staff as possible. Dancing stops briefly at midnight for everyone to enjoy late refreshments. For the younger Royal Family and staff, the dancing goes on until two in the morning. Being well aware that people have more fun when she is not there, the Queen will have left much earlier. Then the pace increases and everyone lets their hair down.

At all royal homes the day goes in stages that revolve around meals. After breakfast, there is no stopping for elevenses. Mid-morning coffee and biscuits are never served, mainly because the Royal Family do not eat between meals. Brunch is unknown to them. The Queen likes to go riding sharp at ten-thirty and ladies can join her if they wish. Anyone who doesn't ride is expected to amuse themselves. At Balmoral there are about six horses available, which are brought up from Windsor by road. The dogs for shooting are transported from Sandringham in a small van. At Sandringham there are both stables and kennels, so none of the animals has to be moved.

After riding, lady guests are expected to be ready to go in Land Rovers to join the shoot, where lunch will be taken at around one or one-thirty. This will be served indoors in Norfolk, or in the open air in Scotland. The entire meal will have been transported by the staff in a van designed by Prince Philip, which very cleverly keeps hot food hot and cold food and drinks cold. Alcoholic drinks are also served, though it is frowned upon for the guns to drink anything intoxicating.

The Royal Family love being outdoors, and every weekday in the summer holidays they eat outside. Even if it's a non-shooting day they'll still have a picnic, and guests are expected to be equipped with wellies and tweeds and not mind the elements. These picnics are very civilized. There's not a lot of sitting on damp grass, as along with the food arrive thick car rugs and shooting sticks, which turn into very basic seats.

Winter shooting lunches at Sandringham are rather more com-fortable – generally eaten in estate village halls, transformed by tables properly laid up with the royal number two silver, and plain white shooting china that goes back to the First World War. All these plates will have been pre-heated at the house and wrapped in blankets to keep them warm.

Lunch over, the ladies then accompany the shoot, walking behind with the dogs. This is an occupation that some of Prince Charles's young ladies before Lady Diana Spencer found very wearing. One or two did not last the weekend!

Those guests at Balmoral who go out for a day of deer stalking will take a small waterproof lunch bag which they sling over their shoulder. It is terribly important to the staff that nobody goes without their lunch, and the lunch bag is checked off along with the guns and the ammunition before the hunters leave for the hills. The bag is packed with a very simple meal; a home-made roll, the top cut off, the crumb scooped out, and then filled with layers of meat. Mutton pies, a traditional Scottish delicacy, plum pudding and something to drink are also provided. The drink is usually lemon refresher, ginger beer or lager, with a small hip flask of whisky to be shared with the ghillie on the hill.

It is a long day stalking, but even so, at Balmoral, those with any energy left have the opportunity to pop outside to the Dee and fish for salmon. It's surprising how many do. Everyone comes home around five for tea, and then follows what the royal family's servants always call the silent hour, when the guests get themselves together for the next innings.

At six the drinks tray is wheeled into the drawing room, and once again guests can help themselves until dinner is served. It's very rare for anyone to get drunk, though on the occasions when it has happened the Queen just pretends not to notice. She *has* noticed, of course; she doesn't miss a thing. If people do get high it's usually because, in spite of the Queen's efforts to put everyone at their ease, they're suffering from nerves. The staff are careful not to give guests powerful drinks, and yet the Royal Family, if handed a bottle and a glass, pour the most lethal drinks for themselves, probably out of inexperience. They don't have to pour their own drinks too often, as there are usually several dozen people about to do it for them.

However, no one has ever seen the Queen remotely tipsy, though it is said that she can get quite giggly when she's happy. But then none of them drinks a lot. The Duke of Edinburgh would just as soon have a pint of lager as a glass of champagne. The Queen Mother loves a dry martini when she is flying, a gin and Dubonnet before a meal, and she also always has a glass of champagne after dinner. Her drinks tray is taken up to her room about five-thirty and she comes down about six-thirty, looking for someone to play cards with her, which she loves. Her game is bridge, but if no one is around she'll play patience.

The Queen Mother has several weekend homes of her own, but Royal Lodge in Windsor Great Park is where she spends most of her time and where she does her entertaining. Much of the basic detail of being a royal guest is the same at Royal Lodge as at Windsor Castle, but not surprisingly the Queen Mother adds her own little touches.

A footman wakes the Queen Mother's guests gently from between cheerful yellow cotton sheets – not by knocking at the door but by opening the curtains before slipping away to draw a bath. In the bathroom towels, a mixture of linen and cotton towelling, are laid out in a variety of sizes and shapes. By the lavatory is a small mahogany box holding about eighty sheets of old-fashioned stiff Bronco loo paper. Happily, soft paper is available as well. The British aristocracy have a saying that it is always possible to tell when a great country house is declining – the writing paper gets thinner and the loo paper gets thicker! At Royal Lodge the writing paper is very thick indeed, and carries the name of the local railway station with a small picture of a train. There is a separate card with the train times printed on it. Yet another card, typewritten, gives the hours at which the staff collect post from the silver salver left in the hall for the purpose. Another very thoughtful touch is that every room has its own supply of Alka-Seltzer and Lucozade.

It is infra-dig when signing a royal visitors' book to write anything other than your name and the dates of your stay. But the Queen Mother, though not wishing for comments, is charmed if her guests can place a small photograph of themselves by their signature in her large leather-bound book.

The great treat for Royal Lodge guests is to see the Queen Mother's superb drawing room. It is indeed a room fit for a Queen, grandly high-ceilinged and full of beautiful things. Yet there are simple family photograph albums placed on a stool, books, green plants, and a homely china frog on the table which make it also a room for living in, comfortable and full of warmth and colour. It is a happy room which reflects the personality of its owner, and it is just as it was before the Queen Mother's husband, King George VI, died in 1952.

In the early 1980s it was completely redecorated while Her Majesty was taking her usual summer holiday at her Scottish homes. The delighted Queen Mother came home to a room in which the colours, the placement of the furniture and the atmosphere were exactly the same as those which she and her beloved Bertie had planned – and later created – when they first fell in love with the house in 1931.

Guests there are very privileged to be invited, because the house is dear to the Queen Mother's heart. From the long windows of the saloon she has a wonderful view of the beautiful garden that her husband – a man who liked to get his hands into the earth – created with her assistance. She has not permitted the garden to be changed in any way from how Bertie first planted it all those years ago.

There are two desks in the room, where she and the King worked side by side. These, too, have been left unchanged, arranged as they were then, as if he had never gone away. The late King's memory is very much alive at Royal Lodge. And every year since he died, still only in middle age, his widow has spent 6 February, the anniversary of his death, at this house, remembering him.

It is in the drawing room that she entertains her friends for drinks on the weekends and special occasions that she spends in her Windsor home. The drinks are carried in on big silver trays by a footman and left for the guests to help themselves. And her guests are a pretty mixed bag, ranging from bishops through her racing staff to the pop singer Elton John.

What very often does surprise first-time visitors is that few of the private royal residences are at all grand. At Balmoral a guest might be surprised to come into the stone-floored entrance hall to find it littered with fishing rods, waterproof clothing, wellington boots and dog bowls. The Queen personally feeds her dogs there.

There is also a collection of ancient bikes left for anyone who feels like a little change of exercise from tramping the moors. The hall is dominated by a bust of Queen Victoria and the red-carpeted inner hall by an enormous statue of her husband, Prince Albert. In fact the entrance is a sort of clean, but cluttered, royal dumping ground, and it is certainly not tidied up because visitors are coming.

At Sandringham the front door opens into a great open area, filled with comfortable, squashy furniture – nothing grand at all. Everything is sensible and cosy, with the sort of chairs in which people are happy to fall asleep after a long day in the open air. Inside the door are a large pair of sitting scales, looking rather like buckets. These were a gimmick of Edward VII's. He used to like to weigh people when they came and when they went – presumably to see if they'd eaten well. They don't do it any more these days, except to amuse the children. There are screens around the door to help keep out the freezing Norfolk wind. There's also a piano for Princess Margaret, plus a table for her on which to play her favourite patience. Another table holds lots of papers and magazines.

The Queen can sit in the hall at Sandringham, waiting for guests or for the Duke to arrive. When she looks out of the salon window, as they call it, she can see the cars come down the drive. This salon goes the height of two floors, with a gallery around it that has little stained glass windows. From her vantage point the Queen can see if the footmen are eating her mints and sneaking the odd drink. There is very little privacy in Sandringham.

But it is here, more so than anywhere else, that the Queen joins in the house party. Her idea of relaxing is to do a jigsaw. She always has a huge one going. Not a modern one; she likes a really difficult landscape, and she hides the lid and puts it together blind. Her jigsaw is placed on two card tables put together with a thick board on top and lit by two Anglepoise-type lamps so she can see the colours clearly. The jigsaw is for everybody to do, but people do hold back a bit, especially if there is not much left to finish and the Queen is out for a walk. There's an unspoken feeling among guests that she wouldn't be too delighted to find it complete. Anyone who wanted to give the Queen a house party guest present could not go wrong by finding a big, complicated jigsaw. Her Majesty would be delighted with the gift.

After dinner on Saturday night the Queen generally shows her guests a brand-new movie. Everyone is expected to attend, seated in comfortable armchairs in a row of about eight. The Queen sits in the centre, Prince Philip beside her. A couple of sofas form the second guest row. This arrangement is all left permanently in the ballroom at both Balmoral and Sandringham, ready for a night at the home movies. At Balmoral stags' heads stare down, and at Sandringham the film is watched along with Edward VII's huge collection of armour which is displayed in the ballroom.

It's all very democratic. The house staff are invited, and they sit at the back on old-fashioned canvas director-style chairs; there is no kind of pecking order. Staff and their families from the royal estates are also invited, as are any young children who live nearby. Everyone can watch as long as they are in the ballroom before the Queen arrives. The Queen's pipe major acts as the projectionist, and an equerry sits in the second row with a buzzer to warn him if the sound is too loud or too low, or if the film needs adjusting. It is, of course, a great privilege to see these films before anyone else. And being in the company of the Queen makes it as exciting as any great London first night – without the need for expensive tickets.

On Sunday the Queen never misses church wherever she may be. Prince Charles, on the other hand, was once staying with friends who asked him if he wanted to attend the local church or go fishing. He chose to fish, saying: 'I can pray when I'm fishing, but I can't fish in church.' Attending church is not obligatory – indeed Princess Margaret, who actually is very religious, very often does skip it and stays in bed. But the Queen prefers her guests to make the effort.

A royal house party comes to an end after Sunday lunch. After everyone has eaten, the Queen herself guides her departing guests back to the drawing room where they are asked to sign the visitors' book. Behind the scenes there has been a lot of activity. While the guests were at church the maids have packed for them. They first have a good look around the room to see if the guest has left the envelope with the £5 tip. If not, the maid and the footman will be hanging around rather ostentatiously to say goodbye.

Everything will have been laundered. Guests go home as clean as the day they arrived – possibly even cleaner, as some visitors to the Queen's homes may have been staying elsewhere. If they arrive with dirty laundry, it will be immediately whisked away and returned impeccably washed and ironed. The men's guns will have been cleaned for them and a brace of birds, boxed for travelling, will have been added to their luggage. It is not good manners to arrive at any one of the royal homes in a car that looks as if it has been driven through a mudbath. People do. Yet they will drive away in a vehicle that is immaculate and polished to within an inch of its life, by courtesy of the never seen chauffeurs. That's royal style!

A typical summer visitor's shooting lunch menu, with all the dishes eaten without knives and on laps:

NO FIRST COURSE

COLD LAMB CUTLETS

COLD MUTTON PIES

COLD GROUSE

TOMATO SALAD　　DICED EGG SALAD　　ROYAL RUSSIAN SALAD

BUTTERSCOTCH FLAN　　BANANA FLAN　　APPLE FOOL

CHEESES

The winter equivalent might be chosen from:

SCOTCH BROTH

POULET AU RIZ

IRISH STEW

STEAK AND KIDNEY PUDDING

TREACLE TART

SELECTIONS OF SALADS AND HOT VEGETABLES

HOT MINCE PIES

COLD CHRISTMAS PUDDING

LARGE SELECTION OF CHEESES

LEMON REFRESHER

SLOE GIN

The hot food is kept in silver dishes which are enclosed in padded containers. Guests are also offered a cold collation if they wish. Sloe gin, served in a sherry-sized glass, is a great favourite with the Royal Family. The recipes serve four to six unless otherwise stated.

POULET AU RIZ

A 3 lb (1.5 kg) chicken
Juice of 1 lemon
1 onion stuck with a few cloves
1 carrot
1 stick celery
A bouquet garni
3 tablespoons double cream
2 sprigs tarragon, chopped
1 clove garlic, crushed

50

For the pilaff:
1 large onion or the white part of 2 leeks
1 oz (25 g) butter
6 oz (175 g) long-grain rice
2 pints (1.25 litres) chicken or vegetable stock
Salt and pepper

Rub the chicken with the lemon juice. Place it in a deep saucepan with the onion, carrot, celery and bouquet garni. Just cover with cold water. Put a tight lid on the pan, bring to the boil and simmer till tender (about 50 minutes).

For the pilaff, slice the onion or leek, then soften it in the butter over a low heat in a large pan. Add the rice and cook for a few minutes. Add the stock. Season, bring to the boil, and simmer on a very low heat till tender (about 20 minutes). Do not stir.

Cut the chicken into portions. Drain the rice and put it into a large hot dish and place the chicken on top. Gently heat the cream (don't let it boil). Then stir into it the tarragon and garlic and pour this sauce over the chicken before serving.

IRISH STEW

This is a firm favourite with the Queen, who has often served it to visiting foreign royalty. As a result many of them, including King Olaf of Norway, have become converts to this tasty dish. It is based on the lamb joint known as best end of neck, which consists of a number of small lamb chops.

1 lb (450 g) best end of neck
Salt and pepper
2 lb (1 kg) potatoes
2 large onions
Chopped parsley for garnish

Bone the lamb (or ask the butcher to do it for you), and put both meat and bones into a large saucepan. Cover with cold water and season with salt and pepper. Bring to the boil and simmer gently over a medium heat for 30 minutes.

Pre-heat the oven to 130°C/250°F/gas mark ½. Drain off the liquid from the cooked meat and reserve it. Remove the bones. Slice the vegetables, then place meat and vegetables in alternate layers in a casserole, finishing with potatoes. Season each layer with salt and pepper. Pour the reserved liquid over the casserole, cover tightly, and cook in the oven for 1 hour or until the potatoes are tender and browned. Sprinkle with parsley before serving.

SCOTCH BROTH

1 lb (450 g) neck of mutton or boiling beef
3 pints (1.75 litres) cold water
2 teaspoons salt
2 tablespoons yellow split peas
2 tablespoons dried green peas (soaked overnight in cold water)
2 tablespoons pearl barley
½ small savoy or white cabbage
2 large carrots
2 small leeks
1 small swede
1 medium onion
Salt and pepper to taste
Finely chopped parsley for garnish

Bone the meat (or ask the butcher to do it for you). Place the meat, water, salt, washed peas and pearl barley in a large saucepan and bring slowly to the boil. Skim as necessary. Shred the cabbage, dice the other vegetables, and add them all to the pan. Bring back to the boil, cover the pan and simmer gently for about 2 hours or until the meat is tender and the peas cooked. Before serving add salt and pepper to taste and sprinkle with chopped parsley.

COLD MUTTON PIES

12 oz (350 g) hot-water crust pastry
12 oz (350 g) lean mutton
1 onion, finely chopped
Chopped parsley
1 tablespoon any cooked vegetables (optional)
Salt and pepper
Meat stock
1 egg, beaten

Pre-heat the oven to 220°C/425°F/gas mark 7. Roll out the pastry, then cut out four cases with a cutter, or shape them round the base of a milk bottle or large tumbler. Reserve a quarter of the pastry for the pie lids. Cut up the mutton into small pieces and mix it with the onion, parsley and cooked vegetables, if you are using them. Add the seasoning. Moisten with a little stock – just enough to bind the mixture – and fill the cases. Cut or shape four lids a little larger than the cases, moisten the edges of the cases and crimp lids and cases together with your fingers. Make a small hole in the top of each pie to allow the steam to escape. Any leftover pastry can be used to make decorative shapes for the lids. Brush with beaten egg, place on a greased baking tray, and bake until the pastry is light brown. Reduce the heat to 200°C/400°F/gas mark 6 and continue cooking for another 45 minutes. Serve cold.

ROYAL RUSSIAN SALAD

Equal quantities of cooked carrots, potatoes, French beans, peas and mushrooms
1 tablespoon capers drained of vinegar
6 small gherkins
4 oz (125 g) lean cooked ham
6 anchovy fillets
Lemon and mustard mayonnaise to bind
Diced beetroot to garnish

Dice all the solid ingredients, or cut them into julienne strips if a slightly chunkier salad is preferred. Reserve some of the vegetables for decoration. Add sufficient mayonnaise to bind the ingredients, and mix together well. Pile into a serving dish and decorate with small piles of the reserved vegetables and the beetroot (which shouldn't be added to the main salad as the colour will 'bleed'). For an extra-special occasion caviare or sliced truffles can be used as decoration.

STEAK AND KIDNEY PUDDING

At the inaugural meeting of the Monday Club – an informal dining club where Prince Philip meets friends – the Prince requested that one of his favourite dishes, steak and kidney pudding, should be the principal dish on the menu. Wholesome and filling, it is a shame that such a lovely dish is not served more often at dinner parties.

Suet pastry made with 1½ lb (700 g) plain flour and 5 oz (150 g) suet
1 lb (450 g) stewing steak
6 oz (175 g) ox kidney
1 small onion, chopped
1 tablespoon plain flour
Salt and pepper to taste
½ pint (10 fl oz) water
1 glass sherry or madeira

Grease a pudding basin and line it with the pastry, reserving enough to cover the filling. Cut the steak and kidney into equal-sized pieces and mix them in a bowl with the onion, flour and seasoning. Place in the pudding bowl, then pour in the water and the sherry or madeira. Cover with the remaining pastry, crimp the edges together, and then put a layer of greaseproof paper on top. Place a piece of muslin or a clean teacloth over the top and tie tightly in place around the rim of the basin. Fill a saucepan or double boiler with water to within 6 ins (15 cm) of the top and place the basin in a steamer in the water – the water should reach three-quarters of the way up the basin. Boil steadily for 6–7 hours, checking regularly to make sure the pudding is not boiling dry. Remove the basin, untie the cloth and take off the paper. For serving, unmould the pudding from the basin on to a plate.

BANANA FLAN

4 large soft bananas
¼ pint (150 ml) whipping or double cream
½ oz (15 g) gelatine
Caster sugar to taste
½ teaspoon powdered cinnamon
Slices of white bread, crusts removed
Melted butter

Mash the bananas thoroughly, whip the cream stiffly, and mix them together. Sweeten to taste and add the cinnamon. Cut the bread slices into 2-inch (5-cm) fingers and dip them into the melted butter. Place these in a single layer at the bottom of a 1 pint (600 ml) soufflé dish. Soak the gelatine for 5 minutes in cold water or according to the directions on the packet, then stir gently over a low heat until completely clear and dissolved. Leave to cool slightly. Add to the banana mixture and turn into the prepared mould. Chill for several hours or overnight.

BUTTERSCOTCH FLAN

6 oz (175 g) shortcrust pastry
7 oz (200 g) brown sugar
4 level teaspoons plain flour
4 tablespoons water
⅓ pint (200 ml) milk
2 oz (60 g) butter
1 teaspoon vanilla essence
1 egg, separated
1 oz (25 g) caster sugar

Pre-heat the oven to 200°C/400°F/gas mark 6. Line a greased tart dish with the pastry and bake blind for 20 minutes, pricking the pastry with a fork and filling it with a few dried beans to prevent it rising too high. Reduce the oven temperature to 110°C/225°F/gas mark ¼. Mix together the sugar, flour and water in a bowl. Bring the milk to the boil and pour it slowly over the mixture before adding the butter and mixing well. Add the vanilla essence and egg yolk, and stir the butterscotch mixture for a few minutes over a low heat or in a double boiler. Pour into the pastry case. Make a meringue topping by beating up the egg white and caster sugar until stiff. Pile the meringue over the butterscotch filling and place in the oven until lightly browned.

TREACLE TART

8 oz (250 g) rich shortcrust pastry
8 oz (250 g) golden syrup
4 oz (125 g) fresh breadcrumbs
1 oz (25 g) butter

Pre-heat the oven to 180°C/350°F/gas mark 4. Roll out the pastry to ¼-inch (5-mm) thickness and line a greased pie dish, reserving a little for decorative strips. In a bowl, mix the syrup (measured with a spoon dipped in boiling water) with the breadcrumbs and spoon the mixture into the pastry case. Leave to stand for 30 minutes. Just before baking, melt the butter, sprinkle it on the tart and cut out strips from the remaining pastry. Twist each one several times and lay over the syrup mixture. Bake for 20 minutes. Serve with double cream or vanilla ice cream.

LEMON REFRESHER

2 lb (900 g) granulated sugar
1 oz (25 g) Epsom salts
½ oz (15 g) citric acid
⅓ oz (10 g) tartaric acid
5 lemons

Put the sugar, Epsom salts, citric acid and tartaric acid in a bowl. Peel the lemons with a potato peeler to get the rind very thin and without any of the white pith, then squeeze out the juice and strain it. Add the peel and juice to the mixture. Pour 2 pints of boiling water over the mixture. Stir, and leave to stand overnight. Strain and bottle. Dilute to taste when serving.

4

LUNCH WITH THE QUEEN

Apart from cosy family lunches, which the royals enjoy as much as the rest of us, the midday meal is another opportunity for the Queen to meet people. And for several years now she has given about four lunches a year when she does just that. The small gatherings of ten specially selected guests are even known as the 'Meet the People' Palace luncheons. In the terms of the world outside the royal circle, these occasions are rather like boardroom lunches given by a managing director or chairman of a company.

The invitation card sent by the Master of the Household to those who are invited to these Palace lunches gives at least two months' notice. The invitation is almost always sent to their place of work, rather than a personal address. This emphasizes the 'business' tone of the occasion. The guests are people whom the Queen really wants to meet, but whom she certainly would not ask for the weekend or even for dinner. (With the exception of state banquets, dinner on their own territory is a family affair as far as the royals are concerned – it is a meal they only share with close personal friends.)

The Queen's Meet the People luncheon guests are often a motley crew, ranging from jockeys to journalists, actresses to artists, and disc-jockeys to managing directors of huge corporations. Actress Julie Christie was a guest; TV chat show presenter Terry Wogan was invited; the governor of Britain's largest woman's jail was asked, along with people as diverse as editors of the most widely read newspapers and opera singers. And there is nearly always one of the Queen's favourite comedians present – though he is not expected to perform.

These lunches are informal by Palace standards, but appear very formal to the likes of us. To stress that this is a business get-together, wives and husbands aren't asked – something that probably causes a

59

lot of grumbling back home, certainly a lot of jealousy, if not a flaming row!

Surprisingly, considering that Britain has a Queen rather than a King, the royals aren't too much into Women's Lib. The chances are that there will only be one lady guest in the group. And ladies are expected to wear a hat, which they keep on through lunch. The Queen eats bare-headed as, after all, she is at home. Gentlemen wear an ordinary daytime suit, and almost invariably a brand-new tie and shirt.

The guests are commanded to arrive at the Palace at twelve-thirty and are given stickers for their car windscreens so that they are let through the gates without fuss. A footman then takes them to the Bow Room on the ground floor for pre-lunch drinks, where they are greeted by the Queen's lady-in-waiting and an equerry.

The Bow Room is beautiful, painted cream and gold, but with very little furniture. People who arrive early can inspect the four display cases – one in each corner – which house some of the Queen's priceless collection of dinner services. This is probably the most public room in the Palace, used as it is as a sort of throughway into the forty acres of Palace gardens at the summer garden parties. But the lunch itself is always held in the 1844 Room next door – the white and gold chamber where the Queen receives visiting ambassadors. Both the Bow Room and the 1844 Room are very formal, not a bit like the royal apartments upstairs which are littered with dog baskets, books, magazines and family photographs. But few people are privileged to see how the royals really live in Buckingham Palace – certainly not those who come to Meet the People luncheons.

On these occasions an oblong table is wheeled into the 1844 Room and set with glittering silver and crystal for twelve. Also brought in are two sideboards from which the footmen serve. The Palace florist does her bit, and by the time the guests, the footmen and the Royal Family are all assembled the room looks less austere.

Once all the guests have arrived – and no one can remember anyone ever being late – the Queen comes to join them, along with the corgis, who as usual stay with her for the entire drinks time and the meal. It will be about ten to one. There's no fanfare of trumpets to announce her presence – not even an announcement. The door is just opened by the page, and suddenly the eight guests will find the Queen and Prince Philip among them. There is a general fluttering of curtseys and bows, and no one is quite sure what to do with the drink or cigarette they have in their hand.

The corgis have quite an important function on these occasions; they give people something safe and innocuous to talk about, while creating a diversion. On one occasion an old family favourite, Heather, was misbehaving, and the Queen snapped sharply: 'Heather!' at the dog, thereby making the opera singer Heather Harper, who was a guest that day, nearly jump out of her skin!

Lunch is served sharp at ten past one. The Palace steward slips into the room, catches the Queen's eye and says quietly: 'Luncheon, Your Majesty.' The Queen nods and then says casually: 'Shall we go in, then?' She leaves a few seconds to give everyone the chance to finish their drinks and get rid of their cigarettes, and then she leads the way into the 1844 Room. The guests are always fascinated at how relaxed she is; the chances are that they are not!

There is a seating plan just outside the dining room, and if guests haven't spotted it the ever-vigilant equerry or lady-in-waiting points it out so that everyone is seated smoothly. The Queen always chooses whom she wants to sit beside, and this most important male guest will be on her right, while Prince Philip has the usually solitary lady guest on his right. People are always somewhat surprised to see that the Queen does not sit at the head of the table. Her place on these occasions is in the more friendly middle, with Prince Philip (or Prince Charles if the Duke is away) facing her.

There is a very definite ritual regarding conversation at the table. Throughout the first and second courses, the Queen talks to the person on her right. When the third and fourth courses are served, she turns automatically and chats to the guest on her left while the pudding and cheese are being eaten. She has now 'done' two people, and perhaps spoke to a couple in the Bow Room while the drinks were being served. She still has six to go. The point of these lunches is that she has some sort of conversation with all her guests. Sometimes, if the meal is going well and it's a jolly atmosphere, she will talk to people further down the table and a group conversation results.

61

The polished table used for the Meet the People lunches has no table linen on it except for table napkins. You can be 100 per cent certain that you will never see paper napkins at any of their homes! The warmed luncheon plates are placed on table mats which carry pictures of the various royal homes – views of Windsor Castle, Balmoral, Buckingham Palace, St James's Palace and so on. Anyone else serving lunch on photographs of their own homes could be thought to be showing off or even slightly vulgar, but the royals get away with it. Like the corgis and the china, which changes pattern at every course, the Queen feels these are talking points for tongue-tied guests.

Once seated, the nervous guests begin to relax a little and take in the livery of the serving staff: scarlet tunics for the footmen, while the pages sport their tailcoats. Unlike in the old days, no one has to wear a powdered wig – something that has been known to disappoint some guests. The wigs, abandoned for the war, never reappeared once peace was declared. Today livery is worn with the staff's own hair – if they have any!

The table gleams with King's pattern silver cutlery, silver cruets and beautiful crystal glass, all engraved EIIR. The Queen has a special pair of cruets for her own use: they are made in the shape of two silver owls, and the eyes are the pouring holes. Each guest has a menu in a silver menu holder. There are no candles on the table at lunch, just very pretty flowers arranged in silver baskets. There are no finger bowls, either, and if there were they would not have bits of lemon or even a rose petal floating in them. Prince Charles has been known to give little lectures about these kinds of pretensions.

Hostess or not, the Queen is still the monarch, and when the food starts to come around the table on magnificent salvers she is served first. There are two pages serving, and both start in the middle and work their way round.

The Queen prefers to help herself to food, and so the pages who serve hand the salver on the left side, with a large spoon and fork, and wait while the Queen takes what she wants. She helps herself to a very small portion – all the royals eat little and often, and her distinctive voice can be heard after every dish saying 'Thank you' to the page. This is one of the very rare times when the Queen actually speaks to the staff when they are on duty, and for a new recruit her clipped but courteous 'Thank you' can be quite a thrill.

The guests are served their meal in the same way – there's no question of handing over a plate with the meal already on it. If anyone is talking too much to spot the waiting page, they are liable to get a little nudge on the shoulder with the salver as a reminder to get a move on and help themselves. While one page is on the left-hand side of the guest, serving, on the right-hand side is the chap who is pouring the Malvern water or the white wine. It gets confusing for left-handed luncheon guests!

At these Meet the People lunches, the staff remain in the room while guests are eating and clear away immediately there is an empty plate. On other occasions – when the Queen is lunching with friends at Balmoral or Sandringham – the empty plates are all cleared at once. Staff go out of the dining room at these two holiday homes and the Queen rings when it looks as if everyone is more or less finished. Once the staff come in, the guests realize they'd better hurry up!

What does the Queen serve her guests? Very delicious food, but never anything too exotic. Soup is never served at lunch, but the visitors might get a particularly delicate mousse or fish in aspic made in a mould for the first course. One of the Queen's favourite dishes to start lunch is egg drum kilbo. This is simply hard-boiled eggs and lobster chopped up and served in a small cup.

For the main course, traditional dishes are always chosen, but curiously never the most traditional British lunch of all – roast beef and Yorkshire pudding. As far as the Queen is concerned this is served for Sunday lunch and never at any other time. She rarely serves chicken to guests, either, though she herself is very fond of boiled chicken and rice. The royals consider that chicken is nursery food, to be kept upstairs. There is one exception: she loves a dish called champagne chicken. This is made with a boiling chicken, boned out completely and then stuffed with a pâté. Champagne is then poured all over it, and it is left to cook slowly. The chef considers this a very cheap dish – after all, he does use a chicken from the Home Farm, and non-vintage champagne.

The main course at one of these public luncheons will probably be either lamb or a veal dish. The Queen herself is very partial to lamb cutlets and also escalope of veal. She enjoys salmon on a bed of rice, and en croûte, and she also likes steak, but for her it must be very well done – almost destroyed. The chef therefore always marks her portion with a piece of watercress so that she and the page know exactly where her helping is on the platter. As an added precaution the page also puts the spoon and fork beside her piece of steak, so there's no chance of a mistake.

One thing is certain: she will never serve messy, difficult-to-deal-with dishes like spare ribs or escargots, and for two reasons. A nervous guest could make a frightful and embarrassing mess of himself with an artichoke or corn on the cob; and something like frog's legs or a red-hot curry might not be appreciated by everyone. She wouldn't dream of serving offal to guests, for instance, in case anyone doesn't care for it.

The Queen herself doesn't like shellfish, for example clams, oysters or crab, though she does make an exception when it comes to lobster. This is a taste she gets from her mother, who adores it, and orders it at least once a week as 'a little treat'. Prawns with their soft shells are considered all right, but are never served in the shell. As scampi is easy to eat it is often on the menu. So the food will be bland, easy to handle and unlikely to displease anyone. For vegetarians nothing special is prepared, but there is always such an abundance of vegetables to choose from, as well as salad, that no vegetarian is likely to starve.

There is plenty to drink, though again people are very cautious, not wanting to go over the top in the royal presence. The Queen always serves a chilled white Moselle or German hock from the bottle at lunchtime – never heavy wines. Some red wine is also offered in a claret jug. The Queen likes red wine very much, but she doesn't drink it at lunchtime.

Salad is always served with the main course, and everyone has a proper plate for this. The Queen places hers at a particular angle if she wants salad, and then the footman brings the crystal salad bowl for her to serve herself. The salads are always already dressed. The Queen doesn't like her salad tossed. A royal salad has the lettuce as a base, and the rest of the ingredients arranged. She particularly likes diced beetroot, and also sliced tomatoes. Grated egg salad is another favourite, and melon balls with apple or pineapple chopped up small. All of these are served on a bed of lettuce. She dislikes potato salad and mixed green salads. There are five or six mixtures which she enjoys, and these are rotated day by day.

The royals refer to plain fruit – like an apple or a pear – as dessert. Everything else is pudding, and both are available at a Meet the People lunch. Pudding is served first as a proper course. Apple flan with cream from the Windsor Home Farm is often on the menu, as the Queen enjoys pastry dishes. There is a particularly sticky butterscotch flan which the entire family are inclined to request – a dish which causes guests with false teeth considerable problems. A favourite pudding is crêpes Suzette. These are made in the kitchen and the chef comes upstairs to deal with the setting alight. He, too, is in charge of pouring the Grand Marnier sauce over the pancakes before two pages carry in the gently flaming finished dish.

Cheese follows, the English way, and then everyone troops back into the Bow Room for coffee and liqueurs. Some of the Queen's Household come through, having eaten their own lunch, just to mingle with the guests – some of whom they are probably quite eager to meet themselves. Now the Queen talks to the people with whom she hasn't managed to make contact before. Once the time gets to quarter to three she quietly leaves, with the ever-attendant corgis pattering around her, as people murmur their thanks and bow and curtsey. Then there is a dead silence, followed by an audible drawing in of breath as everyone really relaxes.

Twice a year inescapably on the royal calendar are two state visits, when the head of state from a foreign power is the guest of the Queen. They stay at either Buckingham Palace or Windsor Castle for four days, and on the Tuesday, the day of arrival, the head of state and most of his entourage are given lunch in the Bow Room at the Palace or the State Dining Room at the Castle. These state visit luncheons are rather grander than the small and cosy Meet the People occasions. Everything is truly formal.

When the visitors arrive, having flown in to Gatwick Airport in Sussex, they are greeted at Victoria Station by the Queen and taken in open carriages, weather permitting, down the Mall to the Palace. There they are led to the Belgium Suite where they will be housed for the three-day stay at the Palace. They get about half-an-hour's free time to freshen up before the state lunch.

In the meantime as many royals as the Queen can muster, plus most of her Household, are waiting in the 1844 Room to greet the guests. Prince Philip goes personally to the Belgium Suite to collect the visiting President and his lady and then leads them to the pre-lunch drinks gathering. Luncheon is served in the Bow Room, which for this occasion is turned into a dining room.

The Queen leads her guests, walking ahead with the President on her right. There are usually sixty seated for lunch, as all the visitor's entourage will be invited. This can make for a lot of people, as third world countries generally bring everyone – just in case of a coup back at the ranch while their backs are turned.

Everyone is placed at round tables – six of them, ten people to a table – each of which is hosted by a member of the Royal Family. Language can be a problem, but most of the time the royals get by in French, which they all speak well. And there are always interpreters on hand for the Queen and the other royals if French won't do. Everyone else, including the Household, has to muddle along as best they can. An awful lot of smiling goes on in lieu of conversation.

Even though it is a very important occasion, the food served will be very light. The Queen is aware that there will be a state banquet that night, and also that her guests will be having tea with the Queen Mother that same afternoon. A lot of eating takes place on the first day of a state visit.

No one lingers over the meal. By three o'clock the entire party is back in the 1844 Room for coffee and liqueurs and the ceremony of exchanging presents takes place. The presents that the Queen is given vary from lavish ones, particularly if they are from an Eastern country – and on these occasions the royals bend the rules about accepting jewellery! – down to something as simple as a small piece of furniture. In return the guests are invariably given a silver salver and a signed photograph of Her Majesty. Honours are also ex-changed after this lunch. Some guests are given honorary knight-hoods, and the Queen may be given the highest rank available in her visitor's country. And that evening, at the glittering state banquet, the Queen and her visitor will wear the sash of their newly acquired honour.

But these grand occasions are few and far between. The luncheon hour is not normally a time when anything much happens in the royal life. When the Queen is at work – and she considers Buckingham Palace to be a workplace – she almost always lunches alone in her private dining room on the first floor. All she eats is a main course and salad, followed by coffee, brought in by her footman. And she usually serves herself from the hot plate that is left permanently in her dining room. Fresh flowers and fruit are sent up to make the table look pretty, but she is unlikely to eat any of the fruit.

On the rare occasions when she and the Duke lunch on their own, the Duke chooses something brand-new and different from the chef's suggestions, or something he may have sampled on his interminable dinners out. They then have what they call an 'experiment lunch'. The royals would never dream of giving guests something they had not eaten themselves, and this way they add safely to their cautious menu. If they like the new dish and it is not likely to offend anyone, it wins a place in the menu book.

Prince Charles and his Princess are not at all interested in eating at lunchtime. The Prince just toys with his food. His idea of lunch is a bit of fish and a jacket potato, or maybe just a salad, though he still does enjoy ice cream. Reports that he has become a complete vegetarian and food faddist are highly exaggerated. He always preferred cold food. As a young man, his lunch was generally either an avocado with prawns, a poached egg tartlet or a small piece of salmon, broken up, covered in mayonnaise and made into a mould.

He has never been one for luncheon parties, and nothing has changed. The Waleses do very little entertaining. In fact, in the daytime they hardly need a chef. The changes are rung between avocado pears and endless egg dishes. Their last chef grumbled that there was a limit to what you could do with eggs after cooking them every day for a week.

Princess Anne, on the other hand, gives quite a lot of luncheon parties to her friends, but they are exceedingly informal. The Princess will probably be wearing jeans.

Sunday lunch for royalty is like that of any other family in the country. They eat completely *en famille* and they call the style of presentation 'all in' – meaning that the meal is put in the dining room, or on the terrace if it is a hot day, and everyone digs in. There are no equerries or ladies-in-waiting, just them, and perhaps occasionally a new girlfriend of Edward's, brought along for his mother's inspection. They don't see a member of the staff until they ring for coffee.

Prince Charles and Princess Diana aren't often at Windsor these days – not now they are so settled in their own establishment, Highgrove, which is really some considerable distance from Windsor. But the Waleses don't go in for the big British Sunday lunch. Roast beef is not served at Highgrove for they prefer much lighter food, though the Princess has a reputation for popping into the kitchen and picking at the staff food. She particularly likes a chicken drumstick. Like many of the British upper classes, she has a young girl's eating habits, enjoying things not too far removed from nursery food.

The Queen, however, still has the full traditional Sunday lunch. At Windsor the food is not sent up from the ground-floor kitchen until the family has assembled in the Oak Drawing Room. The Queen has a pre-lunch sherry, the Duke a weak gin and tonic, and Prince Edward either lemon refresher or a coke. As soon as the page sees they are all together, he sends down for the food. When it arrives, he murmurs either to Prince Philip or to the Queen that luncheon is served. The food is all waiting on a couple of hot plates on the sideboard by the windows.

They eat a small first course – usually a mousse – and then it's straight into the roast beef. Unlike in most households in Britain, where Dad always carves the roast, the chef has already done this in the kitchen. The roast – medium done, never pink – will be beautifully, thinly cut and served with roast potatoes and greens – either cabbage served in small bundles, or spring greens and fresh peas. Nothing is ever frozen. They are all rather partial to an apple turnover pudding, and this is a favourite finish to the Sunday meal.

Lunch takes no more than an hour. Then they're up and straight out, to polo in the summer, or just to look at something that might be going on in the Royal Park, perhaps carriage driving. Unlike many of her subjects, the Queen does not have a Sunday afternoon nap!

Typical luncheon menus might include the following. The recipes will serve four unless otherwise stated.

FILET DE SOLE VÉRONIQUE

CHAMPAGNE CHICKEN

DUCHESSE POTATOES

GREEN SALAD WITH CREAM DRESSING

CRÊPES SUZETTE

ROYAL APPLE TURNOVERS

FILET DE SOLE VÉRONIQUE

8 small fillets of sole
Fish bones and trimmings for stock
2 glasses dry white wine
½ pint (300 ml) water
1 onion, finely chopped
Juice of a lemon
Salt and pepper
A bouquet garni
2 oz (60 g) butter, melted
6 oz (175 g) white grapes, peeled and pipped

Roll up the fillets and fasten them with a cocktail stick. Put the fish trimmings and any bones in a pan with 1 glass of the white wine, the cold water, chopped onion, lemon juice, seasoning and bouquet garni. Bring to the boil and simmer for 5 minutes. Strain. Place the fillets in a shallow pan, pour the fish stock over them and poach gently until the fillets are cooked. Remove the fillets and place in a warm serving dish. Add the grapes to the remaining liquid and reboil until the quantity is reduced by a third. Remove from the heat and mix thoroughly with the melted butter. Take the cocktail sticks out of the sole fillets and pour the buttery sauce over them. Leave for a minute until the liquid has glazed slightly before serving.

CHAMPAGNE CHICKEN

A 3 lb (1.5 kg) boiling chicken
Juice of a lemon
Salt and pepper
1 carrot, sliced
1 onion, chopped
1 leek, sliced
A bouquet garni
2 oz (60 g) butter
2 oz (60 g) plain flour
8 oz (250 g) button mushrooms, sliced
¼ pint (150 ml) champagne or white wine

Rub the chicken with lemon juice and salt and place it in a deep pan. Just cover with cold water and add the carrot, onion, leek, and bouquet garni. Bring to the boil and simmer until it is tender – about 1½ hours, or until the juice runs clear when a leg is pierced with a knife. Remove the chicken, drain and keep warm. Sieve the stock, which should make about 2 pints (1.25 litres). Add extra water if necessary.

For the sauce melt the butter over a low heat, add the flour and stir for a minute or two until all the fat is absorbed and the roux has begun to turn light brown. Add the strained stock a little at a time, stirring well between each addition. When it has all been added, bring it to the boil. Add the mushrooms, salt and pepper to taste and the champagne or wine, and reduce to a slow simmer. Leave for 30 minutes, stirring occasionally. Sieve the sauce and serve it separately. Alternatively the chicken meat can be removed, mixed gently into the sauce and reheated.

DUCHESSE POTATOES

Potatoes of any kind are a favourite of the Princess Royal and have been since she was a child. The Queen also enjoys them, especially if they are fried. Here is a simple recipe with an unusual coating that is enjoyed by both of them.

1 lb (450 g) mashed potatoes
1 oz (25 g) butter, softened
1 egg, beaten
Salt, black pepper and freshly grated nutmeg
Nibbed almonds and dried breadcrumbs for coating
2 oz (60 g) butter and 2 tablespoons oil for frying

Combine the potatoes, softened butter, egg and seasoning. Shape into egg-sized balls. Mix the almonds and breadcrumbs and put them into a large clear plastic bag. Place the potato balls one at a time in the bag and shake gently to ensure they are well coated. Melt the remaining butter and the oil in a shallow frying pan, and when this mixture starts to sizzle fry the coated potatoes until they are lightly browned.

GREEN SALAD WITH CREAM DRESSING

When the Queen was pregnant she used to start every meal with a green salad for health reasons. Today she still eats them regularly for enjoyment. For any salad, only the freshest ingredients should be used.

Cos lettuce, chicory, watercress and endive in proportions according to
taste
3 parts single cream to 1 part tarragon vinegar
1 teaspoon mustard powder
Salt and pepper

Wash the salad ingredients, shake off excess water and place them in
a clean teacloth. Swirl the cloth around – it will absorb the remaining
moisture from the leaves. Tear them into bite-sized pieces and place
in a salad bowl. For the dressing, place all the ingredients in a jam jar
with a secure lid and shake until everything is well mixed. Just before
serving, pour the dressing over the salad and toss gently.

CRÊPES SUZETTE

5 oz (175 g) plain flour
1 egg plus 1 extra yolk
1 tablespoon melted butter plus 2 oz (60 g) softened
½ pint (300 ml) milk
2 oz (60 g) sugar lumps
1 orange
1 tablespoon curaçao
Oil for cooking
Icing sugar for dusting
2 tablespoons brandy

Sieve the flour into a basin, make a well in the centre and add the egg,
the extra yolk and the melted butter, which should not be too warm.
Using a whisk, begin adding the milk a little at a time, beating well.
The final batter should be as thin as single cream. Add more milk if
necessary. Rub each sugar lump over the skin of the orange to soak
up the orange oil. Add them to the softened butter and beat together
until light and fluffy. Squeeze the orange, add 1 tablespoon of orange
juice and the curaçao, and beat again.

Heat a non-stick pan and pour in a little oil. Swirl it around so that it covers the base completely and pour away any excess. Pour in sufficient batter to give a thin layer and place the pan on a high heat. When the edges begin to brown, loosen them with a spatula. Cook for a few seconds more, then turn over the crêpe. Shake the pan if the crêpe begins to stick. Cook the reverse side, then spread on a thin layer of the orange and butter filling. Fold into four and keep warm. Repeat until all the batter is used up. Transfer to a warm, buttered dish and dust with icing sugar. Warm the brandy, pour it over the crêpes and set alight at the moment of serving.

ROYAL APPLE TURNOVERS

1½ lb (700 g) cooking apples
1 oz (25 g) butter
1 tablespoon honey
1 lb (450 g) puff pastry, fresh or frozen
A little granulated sugar
Icing sugar for dusting

Pre-heat the oven to 220°C/425°F/gas mark 7. Peel and slice the apples and stew them gently over a low heat with the butter, honey and a little water until you have a thick puree. Roll out the pastry 1 inch (2.5 cm) thick and cut into rounds 4 ins (10 cm) across. Place a spoonful of the apple puree on one half of the round and dampen the edges with water. Fold into a half circle, press the edges together, sprinkle with the granulated sugar and bake for 15 minutes. Lower the heat to 180°C/350°F/gas mark 4 and bake for a further 10 minutes. Serve dusted with a little icing sugar.

5

A ROYAL UPBRINGING

Princess Diana and Prince Charles's close personal interest in their children, William and Harry, is one of the ways in which the Royal Family are becoming more modern. For generations children were seen and not heard; they lived in the nursery, where Nanny had absolute charge.

When she became pregnant for the first time, Diana made it quite clear that she was having none of this old-fashioned nonsense. Her children would not be locked away in the nursery only to appear in their party best for half an hour in the evening. She considered motherhood and the bonding of babies to their mother – not their nanny – of the utmost importance, and made her feelings clear to Charles. He agreed wholeheartedly and, together, they devoured books on child-rearing. Diana also wanted a nanny with a more modern approach – someone who would assist, not take over – and when Charles suggested that his much-loved old nanny Mabel Anderson might fill the position, Diana was horrified. She told her husband in no uncertain terms that, sweet though Mabel might be, she was far too stiff and starchy for Diana's modern ideas.

Mabel wasn't truly stiff and starchy – she never wore a uniform – but Diana made the right decision in not employing her. It would certainly have meant a clash of temperaments since Mabel, with her years of royal training, could not have adapted to Diana's methods.

After Nanny Anderson left Buckingham Palace she worked for a short time at Gatcombe Park, the home of Princess Anne and Captain Mark Phillips. She was caring for their son, Peter, but she found the household far too informal and was unable to come to terms with the mess of gum boots and dogs in the hall of a royal home, and – worse – the lack of a nursery footman to help her.

Today the royal parents actually sit down to meals with their offspring – once Nanny has instilled the necessary table manners. Unless their parents had total confidence in their behaviour, even today the very young children would be unlikely to appear on any occasion when guests were present, with the possible exception of Sunday lunch. The royals would think it the height of discourtesy to inflict a badly behaved child on a guest.

However, there is grave doubt among the more old-fashioned staff in royal circles as to whether young Prince William is being given the same upbringing and being taught to mind his manners in the way that the other royal children have been. It was thought that his former nanny, Barbara Barnes, was a touch too indulgent with him, and didn't install enough discipline into the nursery. She was replaced in 1987 by Ruth Wallace, who, together with her assistant Olga Powell, who had been there from the beginning, took William in hand – sometimes literally, when the small royal bottom was occasionally smacked.

All the training of little princes and princesses in the past was done by the nanny. When Andrew and Edward were little, Nanny was, of course, Mabel Anderson, who had already brought up Charles and Anne and instilled royal style into them. And Prince Charles adored her. But she was still there after the long gap between the two pairs of children and ready to take over the two last-born princes. She had her problems with Prince Andrew. The staff politely used to describe him as 'high-spirited'. In fact, the footmen were known to give the young Andrew a smart backhander when no one was looking. They objected to him literally swinging on their coat tails.

But there has always been one holy terror in the Palace nursery. Once it was Princess Anne; even earlier, it was Princess Margaret; and today it is undoubtedly young Prince William.

In spite of, or perhaps because of, Princess Diana's keen interest in the development of her two boys, Prince William gets away with more than any other royal child ever has before – particularly when his mother is about. But under Nanny's watchful eye even Prince William will be going through the same routine, which starts as a game. Nanny says to the royal children: 'Come along, eat your greens, and if you're very good you can press that button and a nice man will bring you in your pudding.'

The first thing the royal children are taught to do is ring a bell. And, sure enough, in comes a nice man in scarlet livery or a black coat, and Nanny says, 'We will have the ice cream now, thank you.' And in no time at all the ice cream arrives. The children are not aware that the nice man is hovering outside anyway. But they do cotton on to the idea that, for them, help and assistance will always be on tap to be summoned by bells.

But though life for a royal child is both constricted and protected, they cannot help but grow up believing the world to be a wonderful place. Small royal children get into their parents' car and everyone outside in the street waves and smiles. It's no wonder they believe it's a friendly world. Prince Charles was quite grown up before he realized that all the warmth and affectionate interest in him was because he was different.

In some ways the royals never grow up. The entire family still love childish games like charades and hide-and-seek. Bonfire Night, 5th November, when all British children have firework parties, is another family favourite. The bonfire and firework display used to be held in the garden of Buckingham Palace. Today, with no children left at the Queen's London home, it is Kensington Palace that enjoys the rockets and squibs and Catherine wheels and all the excitement of this particular cold November night that British children have felt for generations.

Royal parents try to make sure that their children are not excluded from the same pleasures as ordinary kids. Nursery tea is in the charge of Nanny and the children are given either milk or the well-known blackcurrant drink called Ribena. Chocolate things are saved as treats, and the little princes are made to eat up their bread and butter before they are allowed any cake. Jam pennies have always been a favourite – but only on Sundays. These are made with great care in the coffee room, and are actually nothing more than a jam sandwich cut into circles with a pastry cutter. The poorest kids in the world could have this royal delicacy, but the little princes think they are marvellous.

Both Charles and Diana, health freaks themselves, are particular about what their children eat. Diana is a champion of additive-free foods. She once discovered William in the larder at Highgrove, swigging from a bottle of pop, and was horrified when she read the contents on the label. Ever since that incident, fizzy drinks have been strictly rationed.

Nursery tea is slightly earlier than for the grown-ups, so that when the children have finished eating they are scrubbed and tidied up to meet the guests downstairs in the drawing room before being taken back to the nursery and their television set. Their television viewing is strictly controlled, and it is considered a treat to be allowed to watch. Princess Diana is appalled by television violence and certainly would not permit her children to watch anything which she thought was a bad influence. But some things will never change. A routine that has survived since Queen Victoria's day is for the little princes and princesses to be brought down from the nursery to the table after grown-up lunch and tea to meet the guests. When at Balmoral they are specially dressed in miniature kilts and frilled lace shirts for the occasion. Nanny escorts them downstairs and then departs. But they don't stay long; about half an hour. It's too nerve-racking if they start rampaging about the Fabergé. Nanny returns for them at six to take them back upstairs for their bath and supper.

The only time that Prince Andrew and Prince Edward came down to tea when they began to grow up was when they were going back to school at the beginning of term. They always came into the drawing room, where their places at the table would be laid up for what is known in the North of England and Scotland as high tea. While the other guests ate sandwiches and cakes, Andrew and Edward would be tucking into a mixed grill of lamb chop, sausages, tomatoes, mushrooms and French fries, served from a silver dish. On these occasions they were the centre of attention and greatly fussed over, as the holidays were over and the time had come for them to go back to being ordinary schoolchildren.

When they were younger, they were allowed to help bake cakes or biscuits in the kitchen. Their efforts would then be served up at nursery tea, with their initials on the biscuits so they knew which ones they had rolled out with grubby schoolboy paws. Edward very much liked helping out. Andrew and Anne were bored to death by cooking. Charles, however, enjoyed these sessions and still likes to turn his hand to cooking – especially old-fashioned soups made from things grown in the Highgrove garden. One of his favourites is nettle soup, but he confesses he doesn't always know when to pick them to avoid being stung. No doubt, in time, his own two children will find their ways to the kitchens of their realm.

Old traditions live on in a royal child's life. At Christmas at Windsor, in the nursery quarters in the Queen's Tower, the children are encouraged to decorate their tree, which has been cut from the Sandringham woods, themselves. The first thing that Prince William and Prince Harry's nanny do on their arrival at the Castle is to get out the crib. Tucked away in the nursery cupboard for the rest of the year, the crib has been dressed and set up by generations of royal children. It sits on a round table in a corridor in the nursery suite. The children gather straw from the Windsor stables and arrange the small china figures of the Virgin Mary, Joseph and the Three Wise Men into a charming Christmas tableau.

The nursery at Windsor is quite large: it needs to be, with so many young children in the Queen's extended family. It has four rooms, a kitchen and two bathrooms. A log fire burns in the day nursery grate, and in the morning the children listen to the guards band playing carols outside the window. As Prince Charles remarked, there aren't too many children who have a regimental band laid on for their personal entertainment on Christmas morning.

In Queen Victoria's day the children stayed in the nursery all through Christmas, very much not seen and not heard. Now each family unit stays in its own tower – Charles and Diana in the Queen's Tower, Princess Anne and Mark Phillips in the Augusta Tower, the Gloucesters in the York Tower, and Prince and Princess Michael of Kent in the Edward III Tower. The children stay with their parents overnight, but are delivered to the nursery quarters for meals during the day, accompanied by their respective nannies.

Easter, too, has its own ritual. On Good Friday morning all the small members of the family are taken to the Home Farm. And there, each clutching a little straw basket, they search for new-laid eggs left by the free-range chickens. Their fragile finds are taken back to the Castle kitchens and given to the Queen's chef to be hard-boiled. Once they have cooled, they are solemnly taken to the nursery by a footman. And then Nanny settles the little ones down with paints and brushes to decorate the eggs with clown faces.

The Royal Family have a favourite spot in the grounds, a sheltered little corner tucked under the garden wall below the East Terrace. Prince Charles particularly likes to sit here if the weather permits, perhaps because, when he was little, his nanny would leave him in this spot in his pram, a net carefully placed over the front to guard against stray cats. No doubt the Duchess's nanny will place the new baby here, too. For the spot is overlooked by the royal nursery, and Nanny need only peep out of the window to check that her charge is safe and sound.

6

TEA WITH THE QUEEN

In Britain tea, the most traditional of all meals, is served at five o'clock, and it is fair to say that the Royal Family are nothing if not traditional! The Queen unfailingly has her cup of tea every day on the dot of five.

In the old days, tea was a courteous method of entertaining acquaintances rather than close friends. In royal circles this after-noon ritual is still regarded as a convenient way to see someone without too much fuss. Taking tea privately with the Queen consti-tutes a courtesy call – one that doesn't take up too much of anybody's time, leaves the decks clear for dinner, and is a painless way of showing politeness to foreign royal cousins or visiting dignitaries.

Tea is, of course, more than just a drink. It can be a feast, and is enjoyed by the Royal Family with great ceremony in an unchanging British manner. It is at their Norfolk holiday home that they enjoy their grandest and most traditional tea parties. The Sandringham holiday takes place in the winter months. It gets dark early, so the men are forced back from the shoot as the light goes. There is no fishing, so everyone settles down in the warm, beautiful, white drawing room for tea at five o'clock.

The meal has all been prepared while the guns are out in the afternoon. The Queen's staff will have set up the ordinary square card tables which every afternoon are pushed together to make a long rectangular table. Each table seats two people, and is laid up individually with Queen Alexandra's tea services on pretty pastel-coloured tablecloths with matching lace-edged tea napkins. Each place setting gets two knives – a steel-bladed one for bread and butter plus a silver-bladed one for cakes. A small fork is placed beside each plate if a gâteau is being served. None of these are special knives and forks saved for use at teatime – they do double duty as bread and butter knives and dessert forks at dinner.

The choice and quantity of food is enormous considering that everyone will have eaten a substantial lunch just a few hours before. The meal starts plainly, with thinly cut brown bread and butter, but with plenty of Cooper's jams and honey in pots to make it more interesting. Very often, looking quite out of place, a jar of home-made jam topped with a bit of greaseproof paper will be set on a very grand saucer, taking pride of place. The Royal Family love to buy at local sales of work, and always support any village fête or garden party on their estates. They genuinely prefer the country and country things to town life, and snap up home-made jams and preserves, cakes and biscuits. And they make a point of eating them themselves.

As well as ready-cut bread and butter, butter is served in earthenware pots for spreading on to a round farmhouse loaf that people cut for themselves. Also for spreading on bread are various fish pastes and meat pastes which have been potted in the Queen's kitchen. These are labelled and changed every day, as fresh potted pastes have a short life.

A good selection of sandwiches is available, all made with white bread and with the crusts cut off so they are soft to eat. The bread, which is made by the local baker (bread-making in the royal kitchens stopped some years ago), is cut with a special machine like a bacon slicer, so that it is very thin. The sandwich fillings are changed daily. There is always a choice of two, maybe either diced cheese and tomato or grated egg, which is very popular. Cucumber and breast of chicken are regulars. The tongue and the ham for the sandwiches are prepared in the kitchens.

Potted shrimps, still in their plastic tub but placed on a fine bone china saucer, are a daily delicacy. These are mainly for Prince Philip, who has a passion for them and eats them with hot, buttered brown toast most teatimes. The other guests are allowed to dip into his pot, though.

For those who are sweet-toothed there are two cakes on the already crowded tea table, placed on silver cakestands and with a silver knife at the side. It's the pastry chef's job to select the cakes that the Royal Family get for tea, and the result is often rather predictable. They invariably get scones, a Victoria jam and cream sponge, and a chocolate cake which also doubles up as a birthday cake when one is required. The pastry chef just makes it to the same recipe and then writes 'Happy Birthday' on the top in icing; diplomatically, one candle covers any age. People cut slices of cake for themselves, and what is not eaten reappears the next day. The chef will trim the remainder, cut off the dried edges and make the whole thing presentable for serving again. The Royal Family do not believe in wasting food.

Sometimes the chef makes little filled pastry boats with icing down the centre, and brandysnaps. These are great royal favourites. Every day he makes tiny little scones which are served wrapped in a crisp linen napkin to keep them warm. These are eaten plain or perhaps with a little jam.

No British tea would be complete without biscuits, and the selection of chocolate biscuits on offer are manufactured by the famous firm of Jacob's. Jacob's also make a special small chocolate finger biscuit which the public can buy in ordinary packaging. For the Queen, however, each finger is individually wrapped in silver paper. Occasionally the pastry chef will make his own very thin flat biscuits, but they are not very exciting and nobody eats them.

The Royal Family and their guests still change for tea; the women take off their tweeds and put on something like a pretty silk dress, and the men, after tramping the fields all day, change into a pair of flannel trousers and a favourite cashmere pullover. The room in which they eat tea is worth dressing up for. Everyone is surrounded by the Queen's Fabergé collection: cases and cases of it, and worth a Queen's ransom.

When Sandringham is full there are usually fourteen for tea; the Queen sits at one end of the table, her lady-in-waiting at the other. There is no formal seating arrangement, so by arriving well in time it's possible to stake a claim on the seat next to Her Majesty.

She is very much in charge at teatime. In front of her is a silver kettle with an ivory handle, which sits on a stand with a paraffin burner beneath. The kettle itself tips forward to pour, and it looks like a rather dangerous arrangement. The contraption is supposed to be balanced, and as they have been using the same kettle since

Queen Victoria's days and there is no family history of anyone being scalded, presumably it must be safer than it looks. In front of the Queen is a silver salver holding a Victorian silver teapot and a china milk jug and sugar bowl. Placed by these is a very long, thin piece of silver that looks like a fine trumpet. Her Majesty blows through this delicately when she wants to extinguish the burner.

She has two tea caddies at her elbow, one containing her own royal blend, and the other, Indian tea. The Queen's special blend is a mixture of China and Indian tea. Made by Twining's, it is packed in a square tin, and is not exclusive to the Royal Family. Anyone can buy it from Fortnum and Mason's.

With all the implements of the afternoon ritual set in place, the Queen herself warms the teapot – considered an absolute necessity to produce a really good cuppa. When she decides the pot is nicely warmed she pours the water she used for the job into the small basin that holds the tea strainer. A hovering page then empties this. She spoons the tea into the pot with a silver spoon, and adds boiling water from her silver kettle. It is doubtful if the Queen has ever seen a teabag, and she would probably not know what to do with it if she did.

On the Queen's right are six cups. She serves only the top end of the table; her lady-in-waiting is going through the same teamaking ritual at the other end, with the same sort of silver kettle, and will serve those nearest to her. If there are more than usual for tea, extra cups are placed on a small side table at the Queen's elbow. She pours and then passes the cups down the table, serving herself last. For some reason the men always get large breakfast cups, while the ladies are given little ones. Prince Philip never pours – it is considered woman's work. Sugar bowls containing lump sugar with silver tongs are ranged along the length of the table, and there is, of course, a choice of milk or lemon.

The teapot empty, the page comes in with an ordinary electric kettle full of boiling water. This modern but necessary accoutrement is kept outside, out of sight, and the page boils it as needed and replenishes the water in the Queen's silver kettle. It never seems to strike anyone as a rum way of doing things.

The Queen loves muffins, so on her left she has a shiny chrome, double-sided toaster into which she pops them from a pile on a plate, handed to her by her page. In the old days they used to toast them by the fire, but not any more. Even so, it's fair to say that toasting the muffins is the only cooking the Queen ever does.

When the Queen is at Sandringham, there is one other tea party that she presides over which is not in the house. It is held a stone's throw away from Sandringham, at West Newton, the local village. Once every holiday she and the Queen Mother attend the local Women's Institute meeting. They are honorary members; most of the regulars are the wives of the estate workers and gamekeepers.

Many of these ladies come to help out at Sandringham – even the Queen has dailies. On this occasion, however, it is the Queen who looks after them, pouring tea and passing home-made cakes to the women who were brushing down her stairs that very morning. Yet when the Queen gets back to Sandringham House, she still has her own cuppa. Her page will be waiting to brew up in her private sitting room, and as soon as he knows she is back in the house, on goes the kettle.

Teatime is rather more casual in Scotland. The Royal Family make their mass exodus in the summer months to Balmoral Castle, where, being so far north, it stays light very late. Tea is served in the same way, and the same ritual takes place, but at Balmoral this is the one meal at which people can be late, or even not turn up at all. There may still be shooting going on, they may have gone to the River Dee to fish, or the women might be out walking.

The Queen will be in her place at five o'clock regardless, pouring for whoever turns up. She does not wait for everyone to arrive: she has her own tea, and leaves after about twenty minutes. The table and the food are left ready and waiting for about an hour, and late-comers have their tea poured by the page on duty. By then the Queen will be upstairs working on the table plan for that night's dinner – just a couple of hours away.

There is no tea at Balmoral on Sunday as the guests leave after lunch, and it is then that the Queen likes to get away from the house if she can. Her page will order 'tea out' for her and her lady-in-waiting. The pair of them set out to one of the cottages on the royal estate. They don't tell anyone where they are going, but the page will have a pretty good idea as they will have asked for the key to whichever one of the far-flung cottages they have chosen for the outing. The Queen's own Land Rover is used, and she drives herself. On these occasions she likes her dogs in the back and keeps a small picnic hamper by her side. As this is private land, it is one of the few places where she can enjoy driving, and she drives very well. If Prince Philip were to come with her he would insist on driving as, like many husbands, he dislikes being driven by his wife. It is fair to say, however, that she is the safer driver.

En route she and the lady-in-waiting will stop off to visit retired estate workers. These outings are never carefully planned, but the workers do know that at some point in the holiday the Queen will appear to see how they are getting on. Not surprisingly, most of them hang about on Sunday afternoons just in case she turns up.

These scattered cottages were built around the estate by Queen Victoria for times when she wanted to be alone after Prince Albert died; some say not quite alone, but with her ghillie, John Brown. The cottages are still not modernized and have no heating or electricity, but several weeks prior to a royal visit the Balmoral housekeeper will have been on a tour of inspection. She makes sure that each cottage has the basic essentials – hand towels, soap, loo paper, candles and matches.

In the Queen's picnic basket there is always a thermos flask full of hot water, milk in a screw-top bottle and, of course, a packet of her special tea. All the food is in plastic containers. She loves playing housewife, and in these little cottages she will prepare tea and then tidy up afterwards. China that has been slightly damaged at Balmoral is shipped to the cottages and used on such occasions. The Royal Family would not dream of drinking from a chipped cup, but chipped plates and saucers are considered perfectly all right for picnics.

There are many other kinds of tea parties in the life of the Queen. At sea she takes tea with a view on the royal yacht. When the weather is good, the meal is served on the Queen's private veranda deck. And very pleasant it is, too, on her yearly Western Isle cruise, to sit in the open and watch the misty hills of Scotland go by.

On cold days the ship's dining room is laid for tea and the Queen, the Duke and their children, plus little Prince William and Prince Harry, all sit down to enjoy exactly the same meal as they would eat on dry land, using china dating back to Queen Victoria and Prince Albert. Amazingly, hardly any of it has been smashed. Even when the ship goes through bad weather everything is locked behind gates so that nothing can fall.

In their own homes, Prince Charles and Princess Diana are much more informal. They often sit in the kitchen for their afternoon cuppa, and drink it out of a mug – but only when they are on their own. They'll often join the young princes for nursery tea. Princess Diana frequently goes into the kitchen to make herself a mug of coffee – she is the only one of the Royal Family who drinks and eats snacks between meals.

Prince Charles enjoys what he calls 'hunting tea'. When he hunts, he will miss lunch and go off with either an apple or a sandwich in his pocket to munch while he is riding. He also takes his hip flask with him. This is the only time he really drinks alcohol, though most of the mixture of Gordon's gin and sloe gin is shared with the other huntsmen. It's etiquette to pass the flask back and forth so everyone gets a tot.

He always comes home ravenous after hunting, and his staff have a special tea all ready for him. It consists of brown bread and butter, two soft-boiled eggs, muffins toasted to an inch of their life, home-made buttered brown scones and chocolate Bath Oliver biscuits, all washed down with China tea.

When the Queen is at Windsor, tea is always in the Oak Drawing Room. This oak-panelled room with its high windows is over the sovereign's entrance to the Castle. It was once the King's dining room but, as it faces into the quadrangle where the public are allowed, the room has lost its privacy. Net curtains would do the trick, but the Royal Family don't like them, regarding them very non-U. Despite that, they have to suffer them at Buckingham Palace to prevent people seeing into the rooms from the high-rise hotels that have grown up around the Palace.

After the traditional Christmas lunch at Windsor comes the traditional Christmas tea, with the entire Royal Family congregating in the Green Drawing Room. For this occasion tea is laid up on round tables, about six to a table, and the small children join their parents.

The usual tea menu is served, except that there is an embarrassment of Christmas cakes of all shapes and sizes sent in by well-wishers and by companies who make cakes. Most of them are seen by the Queen, and all will have been acknowledged, but the majority are then sent on to local children's hospitals and homes. Those that the Queen keeps are not wasted. They will travel with the royal entourage to Sandringham for New Year and the winter holiday, where they will be served, ever diminishing, during the six-week visit. The pastry chef still makes his own royal Christmas cake, plus several for the staff dining rooms. They are traditionally decorated with white icing, snowmen and red paper trimmings – just like in every other household.

But all these tea parties are small fry compared to the three annual parties at which the Queen is hostess to eight thousand people at a time. These are the famous garden parties at Buckingham Palace, held in July, which most of the British public would give their eye teeth to attend. They were started by Queen Victoria as a method of meeting her subjects. Queen Victoria rode among her guests, waving graciously from her carriage. Nowadays the Queen walks and chats with the people, performing what is known as a royal walkabout.

Weeks before the day invitations are sent out by the Lord Chamberlain's office to a complete cross-section of the public. Some go to the tradespeople who supply the Royal Family with various services. Groups of tickets are also given out to many institutions. Quite a lot of Americans manage to get there by contacting the Embassy in London.

Rules, of course, still apply, including a few archaic ones. The one that allows widowers or divorcees to bring only an unmarried daughter as their partner does strike people as being very odd. No girlfriends or mistresses are allowed. Dress on these occasions is very formal. The men sport grey morning coats and top hats, while servicemen are in uniforms – but not wearing medals, so that everyone at least appears to be on an equal footing. The clergy wear

Prince Charles wearing his favourite
sweater guides his youngest son,
Prince Harry, over the boulders.

Alone at last, Prince Charles
fly-fishing in the River Dee.

Diana looks suspiciously over the
River Dee trying to spot the
photographer, while little Harry,
keeps his eyes on the fish.

The Royal Family drink very
little in public, but the Queen
will always raise her glass for
the loyal toast as she did
in China.

Prince Charles downs a
refreshing glass of orange
juice after a hot chukka of
polo. Pimms, beer and
Malvern water are his
favourite tipples during the
summer polo season.

Princess Diana prefers a glass
of champagne or white wine
to almost anything else, but
admitted to developing a
taste for Pimms during
her honeymoon.

Prince Philip samples the
delights of milk straight from
the coconut.

Prince Harry takes a bite from a large strawberry. Nanny is at hand with the tissues should the juice run down his striped T-shirt.

William, watched by brother Harry plays on the antique fire engine during the New Year holiday at Sandringham. Both children are dressed in matching coats, made by one of Diana's designers, Catherine Walker.

Princess Diana cuddles William during a polo match. Both boys enjoy watching their father play polo and feeding his ponies sugar lumps between chukkas.

The newly-married Duke and Duchess of York returning to Buckingham Palace for the traditional wedding breakfast. Andrew gives one of the bridesmaids a hug while a sailor-suited Prince William tugs his sleeve, demanding a kiss too. Fergie is anxiously unravelling her train from the carriage while in the background some of the staff look on.

One of the Queen's summer garden parties on the lawns of Buckingham Palace. The guests queue in straight rows allowing a narrow grass corridor for the Queen and other members of the royal family to mingle with guests.

The Princess Royal explains a point of horsemanship to Princess Diana in front of the royal box during Derby Day at Epsom. Prince Philip appears interested in the form on the racecard, but prefers watching cricket on the television inside the box.

Ascot week is an opportunity for the younger royals to entertain their friends, and here Princess Diana is seen walking from the royal box with Fergies's former flat-mate Caroline Cotterell. On Diana's left is her detective, Allan Peters, his hand appearing to be at the ready.

their finest cassocks or robes, and the women are usually in brand-new dresses, coats and the obligatory hats.

The gardeners will have been working their knees to the bone to make sure that the camomile lawn is like a billiard table – it always is. The flowers will be in full bloom, and flamingos will be strutting on the lawn. It is a wonderful scene.

A Buckingham Palace garden party is divided into three sections – the Queen's marquee, the public marquee and the diplomatic tent. The Queen's marquee has gold crowns on top, the public's has silver balls hanging down, while the diplomatic one is trimmed with gold spikes. At opposite ends of the lawns, two small awnings are erected to shelter the two military bands who play for the occasion.

Weeks before, the order for the ton of food that will be consumed has gone out to Joe Lyons, the caterers who hold the Queen's royal warrant. From dawn on the day the caterers will be arriving with tea urns, pots, thousands of cups and saucers, teaspoons (which usually end up as souvenirs), plus, of course, the food. Outside, on the lawn, rows of tables and hundreds of chairs are laid out. All is in place by two o'clock, an hour before the guests arrive. Then the Queen comes out from the Palace to see that everything looks all right and meets some of the Lyons's waitresses in their black dresses and white starched aprons. She then goes back inside and does not appear again till four o'clock.

Meanwhile, in her own marquee, the Palace staff will have been busy. The Palace florist, Penny Oliver, will have created the most superb flower arrangements, the materials for which will have been sent up from the glasshouses at Windsor. For a garden party, the gold tea services come out. These magnificent urns, teapots and milk jugs are laid out at intervals on long trestle tables. Gilt knives, forks and teaspoons (carefully counted) are laid in place, for tea is served buffet-style. And there is one extra treat: for those who do not like tea, iced coffee is served as well. Pages in black and footmen in scarlet tailcoats are in place by now, ready to look after the royal guests.

All guests are allowed to arrive from 3 p.m., and at four o'clock on the dot the Queen, Prince Philip and other members of the Royal Family appear on the steps to the garden. One band strikes up the National Anthem, and for the next hour the royals mingle. Each member of the Royal Family takes a different avenue of people, meeting pre-selected guests on the way. By some miracle, gentlemen ushers wearing bright buttonholes get everyone in the right place at the right moment.

Around the Queen's marquee, chairs are formed in huge semi-circles for the public to sit and watch the Queen take tea. At five the Queen walks through these chairs to her tent. Princess Margaret calls it 'zoo tea'; they eat while the public watch. The Queen does not sit, but stands at one end of the trestle table, usually leaning with one elbow resting on it, chatting away to either relations or retired members of her Household, who are invited on these occasions. As usual in public, she wears a very bright dress so everyone can see her. In the tent, the lawn will have been covered with some sisal matting, and there are some gilt chairs positioned around in case anyone feels faint. At the entrance to the marquee, at which stand Yeomen of the Guard in their scarlet tunics, a large rug is placed. It is here that, at about five-thirty, the Queen stands while other selected guests and diplomats new to London are ceremoniously presented to her.

All the while the army bands are playing selections from popular shows and light classical music. The two bands are some distance apart, and have a very simple but effective method of communicating with each other. Each flies a flag, and when one of them finishes playing the bandmaster hauls down the standard as a signal to the opposite end that now it's their turn to get going.

Just before six the Queen returns to the Palace and the crowds drift away. The party's over when the National Anthem is played for the second time that day. And what is the first thing Her Majesty does, back inside the Palace? She has a nice cup of tea.

Everything stops for tea in the Royal Household, and if the royal party is at Balmoral or Sandringham, it is held in the dining room. After a shooting party, tea is more substantial and slightly later.

BALMORAL SCONES

SCOTTISH SHORTBREAD FINGERS

DARK CHOCOLATE CAKE

POTTED FISH

BALMORAL SCONES

8 oz (250 g) plain flour
½ teaspoon salt
½ teaspoon bicarbonate of soda
2 oz (60 g) butter
2 oz (60 g) caster sugar
2 oz (60 g) currants
1 egg, beaten
A little milk

Pre-heat the oven to 230°C/450°F/gas mark 8. Sieve the flour, salt and bicarbonate of soda into a bowl. Rub in the butter and mix in the sugar and currants. Bind with the beaten egg and a little milk (reserving a little egg or milk for glazing) to give a soft, but not sticky, dough. Roll out on a floured surface, handling as little as possible, to a thickness of 1 inch (2.5 cm). Cut out with a fluted cutter and place on a greased baking tray. Brush with beaten egg or milk and bake for 10–15 minutes until well risen and brown.

SCOTTISH SHORTBREAD FINGERS

4 oz (125 g) plain flour
2 oz (60 g) rice flour
2 oz (60 g) caster sugar
4 oz (125 g) cold butter

Pre-heat the oven to 170°C/325°F/gas mark 3. Keeping ingredients and hands as cool as possible, sieve the two flours. Mix in the sugar and quickly blend in the butter. This will begin to bind the mixture after a few minutes, and it should resemble the consistency of shortcrust pastry. Roll or press out into the shape of a square and mark into fingers with a knife. Prick all over with a fork, place on a greased baking tray and bake until the shortbread is beginning to brown. Lower the heat a little and continue baking for 1 hour. Cool on a wire rack and store in an airtight tin.

DARK CHOCOLATE CAKE

8 oz (250 g) butter
8 oz (250 g) caster sugar
5 eggs, separated
5 oz (150 g) dark chocolate
Grated rind of 1 orange
8 oz (250 g) plain flour
2 teaspoons baking powder

Pre-heat the oven to 150°C/300°F/gas mark 2. Cream the butter and sugar until light and fluffy. Add the egg yolks one at a time, beating well between each addition. Melt the chocolate in a bowl over a pan of simmering water, and when it has cooled slightly stir it into the butter and sugar mixture. Add the grated orange rind. Mix well. Sieve the flour and baking powder and fold into the mixture. Whip the egg whites until stiff and fold in as quickly as possible. Pour into an 8-inch (20-cm) greased baking tin and bake for 1½ hours or until a skewer comes out clean. Leave to cool and turn out. A chocolate and orange butter icing can be spread in the middle of the cake for added richness.

POTTED FISH

12 oz (350 g) cooked smoked haddock, flaked
¼ pint (150 ml) single cream
Grated nutmeg
2 oz (60 g) butter
2 teaspoons lemon juice
Salt and pepper

Pre-heat the oven to 200°C/400°F/gas mark 6. Mix the flaked fish with the cream, nutmeg, butter, lemon juice and seasoning. Divide between individual serving dishes and dot the butter evenly on top. Place on a baking tray and cook for 15 minutes. Serve with triangles of thin brown toast.

7

A ROYAL DAY AT THE RACES

There is probably nothing in the world that the Queen enjoys as much as a day at the races. And a day at the races with the British Royal Family is one of the most stylish occasions imaginable; something that all the money in the world could never duplicate.

The Queen's own race meeting is held at Ascot racecourse – just a few miles from her favourite official home, Windsor Castle. For Royal Ascot the court moves lock, stock and barrel to Windsor, along with a few selected and highly privileged guests. Some of these, like the Duke and Duchess of Grafton, the Queen Mother's relations, the Bowes-Lyons, the famous banking Hambros and the Duke and Duchess of Wellington, will be close personal friends. But people whom the Royal Family have to entertain as part of their duties are also invited.

Fifteen years ago, those who came to the Castle for Ascot stayed the entire week. These days the house party guests who stay overnight are changed every two days, and there are often more younger guests present; the girlfriends and boyfriends of the young Royal Family are invited to lunch and to stay for the day's racing. The change of pattern was aimed at giving the Queen a chance to expand her hospitality.

At about the same time she also made the occasion rather less formal, as a concession to changing times. White tie and tails for dinner at the Castle gave way to black tie for the gentlemen. However, as both Prince Charles and the Duke of Edinburgh loathe wearing a white tie, it is possible that the change was less to do with coming into the twentieth century as with providing relief for their royal necks.

But not much else has changed. The highlight of the day, both for the public and for the Royal Family, is still the processional drive down the course in open carriages, which takes place just before the racing begins. But when the Queen and her party appear, rain or shine, waving to the cheering crowds, it won't be the first time that day that she has ridden down this pretty course.

Traditionally, immediately after breakfast every morning of Ascot week she and her guests will have been to the royal stables to saddle up. The Queen and her fellow-riders gallop out across Great Windsor Park and on to the Ascot course. Once there, they stage their own race, which the Queen usually wins. And there is nothing to stop them. The Ascot course happens to belong to the Queen – which is another very good reason for her to take a week out of her year to put in a daily appearance there. Royalty draw in the crowds and the money; a day spent at Ascot is not cheap, and the profits go to her Privy Purse – her own personal source of income.

But most Ascot racegoers consider it money well spent for a splendid day out. Ascot week – the third week in June – is as British as the monarchy itself and by far and away the most fashionable of any British race meeting. The men punters leave behind their tweeds and trilbys and don morning suits, either grey or black with matching top hats. They wear a carnation in their left buttonhole and carry a large, efficient black umbrella. It usually rains!

The ladies have a rare chance to dress up in elegant outfits and extravagant hats. A huge hat, a jokey hat, a tiny concoction of feathers and flowers – it doesn't matter just as long as it's a hat. The racecourse during Royal Ascot week looks like a giant wedding party. No horse stands a chance of coming anything but second to the fashion parade, and the leaders in the fashion stakes, setting the sartorial pace for the other racegoers, are the Royal Family and their guests.

Before the racing begins and while the public are arriving and settling down to their lunch, either in the private boxes or one of the many Ascot restaurants, the Royal Family will all be back at the Castle getting into their own finery – the men with the help of their valets, and the women assisted by their dressers. By a quarter to one the Queen will be ready to meet her guests for pre-lunch drinks in the Green Drawing Room. It's quite a crowd – at least twenty-four people, some of whom may have just arrived for the racing and will only return to the Castle after the last race to collect their cars before going home.

Lunch in the State Dining Room is a fairly brisk and quite simple affair, as the royal party must make their spectacular appearance in the carriages at exactly two o'clock: they are never late. They sit down to lunch in their Ascot clothes, though the ladies do leave off their hats and the gentleman put aside their toppers. There is a gentlemen's and a ladies' cloakroom on the ground floor of the Castle where these items can be left.

Everyone connected with the day has to dress. The detectives wear the Ascot rig; the ladies-in-waiting wear elegant Ascot clothes, though less grand and certainly not as colourful as those of their royal mistresses. Ladies-in-waiting are supposed to melt into the background on these public occasions.

Once lunch is over Prince Charles and the other royal princes get their umbrellas and top hats. Then, with their guests, they make their way to the sovereign's entrance where they all climb into a fleet of Rollses and Daimlers (hired for the week) for the short drive into Windsor Great Park. There, in front of selected groups of people – perhaps handicapped men and women or children from a local school – they transfer into the open carriages with the help of a footman. This is obviously a very exciting experience for the first-time guest. The postillions in place, ladies' hats safely pinned against the breeze and with the footmen behind, they then drive through the Park and on to the course. The day has really begun.

The procession jogs down quiet leafy paths and enters the course through what are called the Golden Gates. A ten-minute ride is ahead of them. There are usually five or six carriages, each holding four people. The Royal Family themselves are in the first three carriages, and the remainder contain the more famous of the luncheon guests. They nevertheless still manage completely to baffle the racegoing crowds. The public can never work out who they are, not recognizing some minor foreign royal or a visiting statesman and his wife. More often than not it's raining, and the carriages go down the course with the Royal Family and their guests sheltering under umbrellas. While the other royal ladies may therefore become invisible to the crowds, the Queen Mother, always with the public in mind, shelters under a plastic see-through brolly.

The drive down the course completed, the coachmen then turn

behind the racing buildings and into the Royal Enclosure. The footmen jump down to help the ladies dismount and the Queen, taking the lead, goes in through the covered entrance to the Royal Box. The carriages go back empty to Windsor, while the footmen who had been riding shotgun nip up the back stairs and into the Royal Box, where they are to spend the afternoon helping prepare tea.

The Royal Box, not unnaturally, occupies the prime spot at Ascot – right by the winning post. The Royal Enclosure is immediately below the Royal Box, and it really is an enclosure. The carefully kept lawn is surrounded by railings, and there are two entrances, both guarded by bowler-hatted stewards who let no one in unless they are wearing the right badge. Until recent times, the right to wear a Royal Enclosure badge was strictly reserved for the upper classes. Divorced people were not admitted – nor, indeed, anyone in trade or of dubious reputation.

Today the rules have been relaxed and the Royal Enclosure can become very crowded. It seems strange to think that in the old days even Princess Margaret, a divorcee, would not have been allowed in if she had been a guest rather than royalty. Now anyone – well, almost anyone – can apply for a badge to the Royal Enclosure by writing to the Ascot office before the beginning of April. There is a snag, though – the application must be accompanied by a recommendation from someone who is already a member and the possessor of one of these prized badges.

Though many people can now get into the Enclosure, the Royal Box itself is still strictly off-limits. It is closely guarded by policemen, who have a list of those who are to be let in and given tea. The entrance is at the back of the stand, and inside the lobby the first thing one sees is the central staircase that leads up to the first floor. This is where the viewing area of the Royal Box is situated and where all the action of the day takes place. By the side of these stairs is a lift. The Queen never forgets to say 'Good afternoon' to the nice old lady whose job it is to press the lift button for Her Majesty's guests to ride up to the first floor. The Royal Family never take the lift, preferring to walk, but it must be said that it is handy for some of their more geriatric guests.

Once in the Royal Box, her racing glasses and day's race card already put in place by a member of her staff, the Queen settles down to watch the racing from the front row of the viewing area. By this time more guests will have arrived from the Castle – the short way, by Rolls-Royce and road. These people are mostly the Queen's Household, royal courtiers, ladies-in-waiting and equerries. They never move far away. Their task for the day is to potter around and see who is in the Royal Enclosure. They then inform the Queen if there is someone there whom she knows and who perhaps ought to be invited for tea the next day. The Queen will say: 'Yes, ask them for tomorrow', and the equerry concerned pops back downstairs to check if those to be invited are going to be at the races the following day and, if so, to tell them of the invitation. It's very rare for anyone to turn the Queen down. If the plan was not to be at Ascot the following day, that plan is rapidly changed. On acceptance, the royal machine goes into action and more names are added to the guest list, so there is no problem with the policeman at the door.

Come teatime there is no table plan in the Royal Box, but unlike tea at Balmoral and Sandringham there is no question of just sitting down at the Queen's table. She decides exactly with whom she wishes to sit, and the equerry or lady-in-waiting quietly whispers the good news to those whom the Queen has chosen.

These Ascot tea invites are another convenient way of entertaining as far as the Queen is concerned. By this method, she can see the third- and fourth-tier acquaintances in her life without too much fuss being made. And if there are any minor foreign royalty at Ascot, they can be entertained too.

Everything looks so effortless to the guests, who are usually regulars in the Royal Box, but in fact a great deal of frantic hard work has gone on behind the scenes. Everything that is used to entertain the fifty or so people who join the Queen has to be brought from Windsor.

The work starts the previous Sunday, when the Yeoman of the Cellar and his staff load a lorry with sufficient wines and spirits to last the week. This haul is then driven to the racecourse and locked up overnight, ready for the start of the week's racing. On the Monday, while the Royal Garter Service is taking place in St

George's Chapel, the staff are deployed in all directions while china and cutlery are going down to the racecourse by minibus ready for racing the next day. On the Tuesday itself, while some of the footmen are serving and clearing lunch at Windsor, others go down to the course in the minibus, along with large trays of food. All of these have to be carted into the Royal Box and then the footmen start to lay up the tables.

By the time the Queen's coachman turns her carriage down the course, at about ten past two, all her personal china and silver will be in place. Flowers from the Windsor hothouses – mostly bright red geraniums – will be decorating both the inside and the outside of the Royal Box. The Queen's page and the Duke's page, along with the Yeoman of the Cellar, all three wearing their black tailcoats, will have arrived by road to oversee the afternoon. The footmen will already be busy serving Pimm's No. 1 cup or champagne. Like all British racecourses, Ascot has a drinking licence for the entire day.

The Royal Box itself is rather like a large house furnished in Queen Anne style, with a large tea room at the back of the stand and a spacious viewing area on the other side. At the front the viewing area is glassed in, with raised seating so people can get a good view of the racing; the windows are electric and can be opened up in rare good weather. The Royal Box is highly superior to the other boxes that stand on the same side of the course. The hoi-polloi have tip seats and a small room at the back where, like the Royal Family, they too serve drinks and food. But the Queen's viewing area has comfortable armchair-style seats, carpeting and several television sets for those who would rather watch the racing with a drink in their hand.

The Queen and the Queen Mother prefer to see the real thing, and it is at these race meetings where the Queen really lets her hair down. Her face, meant always to be impassive, shows every emotion. She can look as disappointed as anyone with a £1 each-way bet when her horse loses; delighted as a child when one wins. It's here that the best and the most revealing pictures of the Queen are taken.

She doesn't bet, but she does have a list of tips provided for her by her racing manager, Lord Porchester, and of course her own judgement of horses is astonishingly good. It probably adds to her enjoyment to have a 'pretend' bet, though the Queen Mother is inclined to have the occasional flutter for real. When she wins, the money goes to charity. Members of the Household also bet, but no one from the Royal Box is ever seen trotting down to the tote. Most of them have accounts with bookmakers and their bets are all placed before they leave the Castle. It would not be considered good form for anyone in the Queen's party to be seen publicly betting.

Prince Philip cannot abide racing: he only goes to Ascot under protest, because it is a royal occasion and the Queen expects it of him. But no one will ever see the Duke watching the racing. He spends the afternoon in the sitting room below the viewing room, with another television set – watching cricket. Officially he is supposed to be getting on with paperwork!

The high spots of the day for the crowds – and Ascot in Ascot week is terribly crowded – is when the Queen and the other members of the Royal Family leave the Royal Box and walk through them to the Paddock. There, along with all the other racegoers, they inspect the horses. They do this several times a day, and their progress is enough to give an FBI man screaming nightmares. The spectators are inches away, just parting enough to let the Royal Family through without jostling them. All anyone just a few feet behind can see of the Queen or Princess Diana are their hats bobbing in a sea of other hats! Security is always there, but it's very hard to spot.

Tea is usually served after the fourth race. If the Queen has a runner in the fifth or sixth it is interrupted for her to get up and to watch her horse run.

The tea room is over the entrance to the box, and looks down on the back of the racecourse. It is a fine room, four windows wide, which can seat fifty at round tables each taking six to eight people. On this occasion the Queen does not pour as she does with her house guests, nor do people help themselves. Tea is waited by footmen. The Queen's page pours her tea, and brings her the traditional food – little sandwiches, kept in see-through plastic boxes, raspberries or strawberries and ice cream together with great blobs of fresh cream from the Windsor Home Farm.

The tea service is beautiful plain white china with gold bands around the edges, engraved EIIR. The soft fruit and truly delicious ice cream, made by the pastry chefs at the Castle, are served in lovely Victorian pinky coral smoked glass bowls with VRI (for Victoria Regina I) engraved on them. This is the only occasion on which the Queen serves fruit and ice cream to her guests, though she loves ice cream herself.

All the leftover food is taken back to the Castle at the end of the day, where it is greatly enjoyed by the staff. There would be no point keeping it, since the Queen insists that, for Ascot week, fresh cakes and sandwiches are made every day.

Prince Charles did not immediately take to 'the sport of kings', but he changed his mind when he bought two racehorses of his own and when he started hunting. He now enjoys watching the racing with his mother and grandmother. But until then he too used to vanish downstairs to the small sitting room where his father lurks and from where neither of them could be prised.

This refuge is a rather dismal, pale green-painted dark room, with two desks, one in each corner. The most important piece of furniture is a long mirror which all the Royal Family use to make sure they are properly dressed before they go out in front of the crowds. Very heavy net curtains cover the windows to stop people peering in, as it is also used as a changing room.

Even in the days when Prince Charles was not too keen on racing, he always very dutifully turned up to the meetings without moaning too much. Once, when he was in the Navy, he had promised that he would try to get to Ascot. He made it, but arrived so late that the royal carriages were already in procession. It struck him that it might be fun to watch his family go past and surprise them by waving at them, then go back to the Castle to change, as he was still in his naval uniform. He went to the far end of the racecourse and waited for the carriages to come round. Suddenly he was aware of someone shouting at him and waving wildly.

'You can't stay there,' one of the racecourse officials was bellowing.

'I kept saying it's only me, but he wouldn't take any notice,' the Prince said afterwards. 'But as he neared, he realized his mistake, and suddenly all the shouting turned into an awful lot of bowing. . . . I don't know why I bothered anyway,' he added. 'They all turned and looked the other way when they got to where I was, so nobody saw me anyway.'

As much as the Prince now likes racing, polo is still his favourite sport. On Ascot week mornings, while his mother and her guests are riding over the racecourse, he will have been practising on one of his polo ponies on the golfcourse at Windsor. And immediately before the last race of the afternoon is run he goes downstairs and changes into his polo gear, ready to take part in the polo tournament that runs throughout Ascot week. Princess Diana likes to watch her husband on the polo field, so the two of them slip away before the last race is over. Prince Charles's open-topped Aston Martin is waiting outside for them to make the dash to Smith's Lawn, the polo field, which is less than a ten-minute drive away. Up until recently Prince Philip used to leave early, too, so that he could referee the tournament.

The rest of the royal family stay for the whole meeting, and at around five-thirty a large crowd begins to gather round the entrance to the box. They know it's a chance to catch another glimpse of the Queen and her party before they leave. This time the Royal Family return to the Castle by car, though sometimes the Queen, too, will stop off at Smith's Lawn to watch her son play.

It's been a very horsy day.

A picnic at the races might well include:

MINCED CHICKEN AND CUCUMBER SANDWICHES

CHEESE STRAWS

CHOCOLATE PROFITEROLES

STICKY GINGER CAKE

BROWN BREAD ICE CREAM

ICED COFFEE

MINCED CHICKEN AND CUCUMBER SANDWICHES

Cooked chicken, minced
Mayonnaise
Mango chutney
Salt and pepper
Butter
1 cucumber
Fresh brown and white bread, thinly sliced and buttered

Cut the crusts off the bread slices. Mix the chicken with the mayonnaise, a little chutney, salt and pepper and sufficient softened butter to make a spreadable paste. Spread it fairly thickly on to a slice of white bread. Cover with a brown slice, butter side up. Peel and thinly slice the cucumber and lay slices on the brown bread. Cover with a white slice and then cut each sandwich into three fingers.

CHEESE STRAWS

8 oz (250 g) plain flour
½ teaspoon salt
½ teaspoon cayenne pepper
4 oz (125 g) cold butter
4 oz (125 g) cheese, grated
Beaten egg for glazing

Pre-heat the oven to 200°C/400°F/gas mark 6. Sieve the flour with the salt and cayenne. Cut the butter into small pieces and rub lightly into the flour until the mixture resembles breadcrumbs. Mix in the cheese, and moisten with sufficient cold water to bind into a stiff dough. On a floured surface roll out the dough to ½-inch (1.5-cm) thickness. Cut into ½-inch (1.5-cm) strips and twist two or three times. Brush with beaten egg and bake for 10–15 minutes.

CHOCOLATE PROFITEROLES

Chocolate profiteroles have a firm place in royal history. They were served to twenty-six of the Buckingham Palace Brownie Pack by a young Princess Anne one Christmas, and Prince Andrew and Sarah Ferguson are reputed to have fallen in love over a plate of them when Andrew tried to 'force-feed' a dieting Fergie.

For the choux pastry:
½ pint (300 ml) water
4 oz (125 g) butter
2 oz (60 g) caster sugar
½ teaspoon salt
4 oz (125 g) plain flour
A few drops vanilla essence
2 eggs

For the sauce:
2 oz (60 g) plain chocolate
½ oz (15 g) butter
2–3 tablespoons water

Whipped cream to fill

Pre-heat the oven to 200°C/400°F/gas mark 6. For the pastry put the water, butter, sugar and salt into a saucepan and gently bring to the boil. Then sieve all the flour into the pan at once, stirring well, and leave to cook gently for at least 10 minutes or until the mixture comes easily away from the sides of the pan. Let it cool a little, then add the vanilla essence and beat in the eggs one at a time. Put the pastry into a piping bag with a large plain nozzle. Pipe 5-inch (13-cm) lengths on to a greased baking tray and bake for about 25 minutes until well risen, crisp and golden brown. When cooked, place on a cooling tray and slit the side of each one to let the steam escape.

To make the sauce place the chocolate, butter and water in a small basin over a pan of simmering water and stir until melted. When the cooked profiteroles are cold, fill the slit along the side of each with the

whipped cream, using a piping bag or teaspoon. Spread the chocolate sauce over the top and leave until set.

   Do not fill the profiteroles too long before serving or they will go
soft.

STICKY GINGER CAKE

6 oz (175 g) butter
6 oz (175 g) soft brown sugar
2 eggs, beaten
2 oz (60 g) treacle
10 oz (300 g) plain flour
½ teaspoon bicarbonate of soda
1 teaspoon ground cinnamon
2 teaspoons ground ginger
3 oz (90 g) walnuts
6 oz (175 g) sultanas
A little milk

Pre-heat the oven to 180°C/350°F/gas mark 4. Cream the butter and
sugar together until light and fluffy. Add the eggs one at a time,
beating well between each addition, then add the treacle. Sieve the
flour with the soda and spices, and fold into the mixture. Add the
nuts and fruit. The mixture should then be of a consistency which
will just fall off the spoon. If it is too dry, add a little milk. Turn into a
greased tin lined with greaseproof paper and bake for 2 hours or until
a skewer poked into the centre of the cake comes out clean. Leave to
cool, then turn out on to a rack.

BROWN BREAD ICE CREAM

This particularly delicious ice cream goes down well at any outdoor event. The sugared breadcrumbs stay crunchy and give a pleasant contrast of textures with the smoothness of the ice cream.

1 pint (600 ml) milk
4 egg yolks
4 oz (125 g) caster sugar plus 2 tablespoons
¼ pint (150 ml) single cream
6 oz (175 g) brown bread

Place the milk in a saucepan and heat almost to boiling point. Beat the egg yolks and pour the milk over them, stirring constantly. Return to the pan and stir over a low heat. Do not let it boil or the custard may curdle. Stir in the 4 oz (125 g) of sugar and heat for a little longer. Sieve, leave to cool, then stir in the cream and freeze. Remove the crusts from the bread and crumble it by hand or in a blender. Place in a thin layer on a baking tray and sprinkle with the remaining 2 tablespoons of sugar. Put in a hot oven for about 5 minutes, shaking the tray occasionally. Keep checking, as the bread burns very easily and will become inedible. When it is golden brown and crunchy, cool and fold it into the partially frozen ice cream. Return the ice cream to the freezer and leave until solid.

ICED COFFEE

2 oz (60 g) ground coffee
Sugar to taste
Whipped cream or vanilla ice cream to serve

Brew the coffee as normal. Add the sugar and leave to cool. Just before serving put some ice cubes in a glass jug and pour the coffee over them. Serve in tall classes with a spoonful of whipped cream or ice cream on top.

8

DINING ROYALLY

It takes a considerable stretch of the imagination to accept that the Queen of England enjoys a TV dinner just like the rest of us. But she does – though it must be said that even a TV dinner when taken in Buckingham Palace is still pretty formal. There's no slumping in an armchair, with a tray precariously perched on one's lap. Nor is the food something straight out of the freezer, hastily rejuvenated in the microwave. The meal will be beautifully prepared by the Queen's chef, sent up from the kitchen in a large heated trolley and served by the Queen's page from silver dishes on to one of the Queen's favourite bone china dinner services.

At Buckingham Palace the television set is kept in the Queen's sitting room, and as the Royal Family simply never eat off their laps, they have their meal served in the Queen's dining room, but with the door through to the sitting room left open so they can watch the programme. The TV is the biggest size it is possible to buy, and kept on wheels. No one attempts to hide it in a cupboard or disguise it in some way. The Queen's TV is a very visible object: the Royal Family think that any object masquerading as something else is rather vulgar.

At Buckingham Palace, when dining privately, it's always just family. In London, the Queen never has more than three for dinner, a group consisting of herself, the Duke and the young Prince Edward – and even this is only on the rare occasions when Edward is home and her husband is not attending a formal dinner. Of course, before her other three children married dinner at the Palace consisted of a larger group. The Queen, like any other mother, is experiencing her children gradually leaving the nest. Eating alone, then, the Queen could look out of her windows across to Park Lane, and the chances are that her husband would be dining and speaking at any one of its great hotels. Yet it is only at Buckingham Palace that the Queen ever eats without any company. At all the private royal homes she usually has either family or house guests staying, and then dinner becomes something of an occasion.

But given the opportunity to dine with each other and no one else, the Queen and the Duke are perfectly content. This long-married couple get so little time together that a meal in each other's company is still something of a treat. So when it's just them at Windsor Castle, settling for a TV dinner, the Queen and her husband sit at a table in her private dining room. They both face the TV set, which is on the magnificent sideboard placed to the right of the fireplace – incidentally, one of four open fires that are still lit in Windsor Castle. The Queen has the side of the table which leaves her with her back to the window; the Duke sits on her right. The Queen likes to sit with the light behind her – not for reasons of vanity, but, since she now has to wear glasses for reading, to save her eyes. She is not a vain woman, or like her husband she would have taken to contact lenses long ago.

At Windsor, on quiet weekends in the summer, if the weather is good they have both lunch and dinner on the East Terrace under an awning, disturbed only by the constant roar of planes landing at Heathrow Airport. The Castle is right on the flight path, and pilots use the huge medieval building as a landmark. The noise can be appallingly intrusive, so it's no wonder the Queen and Duke don't bother with the TV set for these outdoor meals. They wouldn't be able to hear it!

Unlike the Queen, the Duke dislikes eating alone, and if the Queen is away he will always invite a member of his Household to dine with him. But the Queen's idea of bliss is to eat alone and extremely simply. She makes herself a very small jug of dry martini, leaving the ice in, and carries it through from her sitting room into the dining room. One small course – probably lamb cutlets, with all the fat trimmed off – will be waiting on a hotplate. She helps herself, and settles down to eat at the table. While she eats she reads official papers.

She never bothers with wine when alone, but lets her dry martini melt down and sips at it. Her meal will be just the one course and a salad, maybe followed by an apple. If the children are home, she will then order a pudding, but if they are not she doesn't bother.

Even if she is eating alone she takes the trouble to change. On a private weekend at Windsor both she and the Duke still change for dinner, but they do not dress too smartly. The Queen will wear a short dress, the Duke a cardigan or a pullover and flannel trousers. He always showers and changes in the evening. The Queen changes her clothes but prefers to have her second bath of the day before she goes to bed.

Personal entertaining is out at Buckingham Palace, the Queen's workplace. Most of her closest friends are country people, but if they came up for an evening in town not one of them would dream of ringing up to beg a bed for the night. The Palace has plenty of spare bedrooms, but not, the Queen feels, to house her personal friends or even foreign royalty. Buckingham Palace does not belong to her. It belongs to the nation, and the nation pays for its upkeep.

All her personal entertaining, therefore, is done in the long summer and winter holidays at Balmoral and Sandringham. And at dinner she serves a completely different menu from the lunchtime one. Dinner dishes are more elaborate and richer in ingredients and sauces. The Royal Family never have game for lunch, for example, but for friendly dinner parties it is almost always on the menu – providing the men have shot sufficient during the week, and it's very rarely that they haven't.

In a world that becomes increasingly less glamorous, dinner with the Queen at one of her private homes is a marvellous reminder of how much more gracious life once was. The table is always lit by candles. If it is just family, there will be four tall candles in single candle-holders. The candelabra, sometimes as many as four, depending on the number of diners, are brought out for larger dinner parties. Sometimes the Queen will ask for ivory candles, sometimes for red or deep pink. Each flame is protected by a small shade on a frame, which creates a warm glow and prevents the wax smoking. Apart from concealed strips illuminating the pictures, there is never any other light in the room. Very beautiful the dining table looks with the polished silver, crystal and porcelain gleaming in the soft candlelight.

The Queen always wears a long dress with diamond earrings and a matching necklace for formal dinners. The dress will be one that has done its duty on royal tours, and has now been put into private service. Contrary to popular belief, the Queen does not wear her clothes only once or twice. They never get shabby, and they are never thrown away. There are cupboards and cupboards in Buckingham Palace where the royal wardrobe, going back over many years and generations, is stored.

Naturally, all the guests are expected to dress accordingly, and dinner is a splendid sight. It is only about twelve years since ladies still wore gloves at table, but etiquette decrees that tiaras and gloves are a twosome, and when it was no longer considered necessary to wear tiaras for dinner, out went the gloves as well. Now the only time the Queen wears one of her splendid collection of tiaras at dinner is at a state banquet (with long white gloves), or if she has guests on the royal yacht on a state occasion, as in the case of President and Mrs Reagan in California. The royal ladies also wear them on the night of the two ghillies' balls at Balmoral. It is not a truly formal occasion, but the Queen likes to pay her Scottish staff the compliment of dressing to the nines.

These days, wherever dinner is being served the men wear dinner jackets and black tie, or in Scotland those who are entitled by birth wear the kilt. If the party is taking place at Windsor Castle in the State Dining Room, Prince Charles and Prince Philip wear what they call the Windsor coat. This is a dinner jacket based on a hunting design, in navy blue with a red collar and cuffs, modelled on one that George III created to be worn at Windsor back in the late eighteenth century.

At Windsor, incidentally, the guest list is often increased when the Queen invites the officer of the guard from the Windsor barracks to attend dinner. This makes a good opportunity for the Queen and her family to meet any new guards officers who have recently joined whichever regiment is stationed at the Castle.

Dressing for dinner was once much more formal, with the men sporting both tails and decorations. It's only recently that a dinner jacket without decorations has become acceptable, even at Ascot week, which was always the grandest and most dressy private week of the year.

A lot of things changed during the terrible fuel crisis in Britain in the early seventies. The Queen felt she had to be seen doing her bit and cutting back like the rest of her subjects. Like the rest of the British she did go without heating, and did all her paperwork wearing her mink coat to keep warm!

But not a great deal changes in the Royal Family's routine. You could set your watch by the time they eat their meals, and the precision with which the staff ensure they arrive is a marvel that never falters. Everything is done according to tradition. They have a number of different ways even for setting a table. When the Queen is on her own the cutlery for the whole meal is put in place. If there are just two of them eating, they help themselves to food from a hotplate. The Queen's rules are that there have to be more than two before she is waited on.

At formal dinners, the cutlery is put down for the first and second course and then the footmen 'crumb' – wipe down the table with a napkin on to a small silver salver – before putting down the cutlery separately for the pudding or savoury and dessert. This is exactly the same procedure as in a good restaurant, whereas at lunch all the silver is put in place from the start of the meal. Butter is served individually to each guest at dinner – everyone has their own little glass dish with a couple of pats. Salt and pepper cruets are also a pair per person, with a set put in front of each place setting. When dessert – bowls of apples, pears, peaches or grapes – is handed by the footmen, each dinner guest is given a finger bowl on a gilt dessert plate with a gilt knife, fork and spoon. These are set just to the left of the place setting. The guests then lay out their own cutlery for the fruit course.

Some of the Queen's china is very old indeed, though much of her collection consists of wedding presents from when she and Prince Philip were married in 1947. She is very interested in fine china, and every formal printed menu tells the make and pattern of the china used for each course. This gives people a chance to see the Queen's collection, but there is also another consideration. The china does make a talking point with a very dull guest, and some of the Queen's duty guests can be very dull indeed.

But what about the food? Dinner always starts with a hot fish dish – perhaps fried scampi diced up with breadcrumbs, or a scampi

113

mornay. The chef might make a rice mould and fill it with diced white fish covered in various sauces. Very often, particularly at Balmoral where the river runs outside the front door, there will be a salmon starter – perhaps a salmon quiche. Another favourite is a celery heart wrapped in a thin slice of ham and covered with cheese sauce. Soup is hardly ever on the menu (though, surprisingly, it is served at state banquets). Only the children in the royal nursery are given soup for their supper, served in lovely little earthenware pots with lids.

The grown-ups are invariably given game. Pheasant or partridge are served virtually every night at Sandringham during the winter holiday, and grouse is almost always on the menu every night at Balmoral and every night at the Queen Mother's home, Birkhall, on the Balmoral estate. This sends the chef into despair. How many ways can you cook a grouse! The Royal Family do not hang the birds for too long – rarely more than a couple of days. They don't like the meat to be very 'high' as in so many British country homes, especially as well-hung game is an acquired taste which not all their guests might appreciate. They are also aware that there are people who do not care for game at all, and therefore one of the page's jobs at both Balmoral and Sandringham is to catch the guests after tea to ask if they would rather have chicken for dinner. A good many of the ladies settle for the farmyard variety of bird.

While the page is asking his questions, the Queen is working out the evening's seating plan, which she then passes to him. It is his duty to mark beside each guest's name what they wish to eat. This avoids 'Chicken or grouse?' questions once everyone is seated at table. Come dinner, the footmen know how to follow through. They know that those who are having game are served with fried breadcrumbs, and that those who are eating chicken are to be given bread sauce, and of course they offer the two different gravies.

Salad, always served with dinner, is the Queen's prop. As it is not polite for anyone to be eating after she has finished, if one of her guests (and it's usually Prince Charles) is slow, she keeps a fork in her hand and toys with her salad until the moment is right to ring for the staff to come in and clear. The electrically wired bell, which she personally presses, is most discreetly hidden immediately under the table at her place.

For a third course, lucky guests are served with either a sweet or savoury soufflé. The Queen really likes these – either chocolate or cheese or, a special favourite, a very mild kipper soufflé. Royal soufflés rarely sink, but in case of emergencies the chefs always make an extra one to keep in reserve. Soufflés can burn as well as sink, and some butter-fingered footmen have been known to drop them. Sixteen for dinner means not four, but five, soufflés rising, hopefully on time, in the rather old and unreliable ovens. It is one of the few dishes that the Queen will sit and wait for. If all goes well, the staff get the spare one, and the senior staff make a beeline for the kitchen on the days when soufflés are on the menu. Why not? Soufflés don't keep, so someone might as well eat them.

There's a very strict rule – which is constantly broken – that no dish must be touched after it has left the table. If there is a piece of grouse or salmon left over it is supposed to be taken to the kitchen to be 'recycled'. However, one or two of the pages who are on dinner duty don't bother to go to staff supper; they know that there'll be a portion of something delicious left over. After the Queen's bell has gone for the staff to clear, a fly on the wall would see one or two of the older pages gulping down their clandestine dinners in the silver pantry, while waiting for the bell to go again. Naturally they are always a course behind the royal table, and undoubtedly the Royal Family know exactly what is going on and, unlike Queen Victoria, are probably rather amused.

The Queen has a sweet tooth and for family meals loves chocolate Dalmatian ice cream for pudding, served in bowls with scoops. This is plain vanilla ice cream with mint chocolate chips in it, and looks rather like a Dalmatian dog. The Queen believes she invented it, not knowing that it has been on sale for many years in the USA. Another favourite, which is also served when there are guests, is a bombe, meringue-covered ice cream piped with thick cream; as an added refinement the chef breaks up chocolate mints and uses them as decoration. One rule of royal style is that cheese is never served at dinner.

Even today the ladies still leave the room after dinner to 'powder their noses', as going to the bathroom is euphemistically called even in royal circles. Needs of nature taken care of, they head for the drawing room (the sitting room is strictly for the Queen's private use in all her homes) where they gossip, play the piano or help themselves to surprisingly manly drinks, like scotch, brandy or vodka, from a tray.

While still at the table, the men pass around the Taylor's vintage port, always from the right (it is considered unlucky to ever pass the decanter anti-clockwise – an old British naval superstition). The port itself will have been a gift presented to the family many years ago on some royal occasion and laid down in the royal cellars ever since.

Over the years the length of time before the men joined the ladies has become shorter. And in Princess Diana's home it is no more than a brief formality. A modern girl, she probably thinks the separation antiquated. The Prince and Princess lead much quieter social lives than the Queen and hardly entertain at all. When they married, the Princess had her wedding present lists at the General Trading Company in London's Sloane Street. She wanted some very pretty china with a pattern of bows and butterflies, and was given masses of it. They were also given a rectangular polished dining table and twelve chairs, and they received place mats, candelabra and some very nice plain silver cutlery with Prince of Wales feathers on the handles. It's sad that they don't use them more, but hardly anyone is invited, because, the Princess says, with their busy working schedules they find it difficult to be at home together at the same time.

They do very occasionally entertain people like the Westminsters; the Duchess of Westminster is much the same age and a close friend of the Princess's. They see a fair amount of Lord Mountbatten's grandson, Lord Romsey, and at Highgrove they see the Prince's hunting friends. All the means to entertain are there. The Prince employs a butler, a footman and an orderly, a Gurkha soldier who can't speak English but is very pleasant. (The Prince is the Colonel-in-Chief of the Gurkha regiment.) The menus the Princess serves her guests are basically much the same as the Queen's. Mervin, the Waleses' chef, was Palace-trained.

The Princess Royal is quite the most casual of the family and very often has her and her husband's dinner served on a tray. They'll both sit on low stools and watch television while they eat. She won't cook the food herself – neither of them ever cooks in the home – though they do like to fiddle about with the barbecue out-of-doors. And neither of them ever washes up.

Princess Margaret loves entertaining and is known for giving the best and most generous staff party every Christmas. The Queen Mother usually has dinner on her own, unless she's going out, which she loves and does frequently. But within reason, most of the Royal Family can choose to be as private as they like. The Queen is not so fortunate. There are so many people she must entertain. Nor is she always in the position of picking her table companions – many of them are duty guests.

Those invited to Dine and Sleep at Windsor are cabinet ministers, ex-Prime Ministers and high-ranking civil servants. During the Easter visit the Queen gives one or two of these evenings a week.

At least eight people are invited, along with their spouses. A problem with Dine and Sleep in this vast castle is that guests are always getting lost, and one night certainly isn't long enough to get to know their way around. The Queen is aware of this, and the guests – who arrive at about six-thirty – are fetched from their quarters by a page after they have had time to freshen up, and then taken down to the Green Drawing Room where drinks are served. They go to the State Dining Room for dinner itself, which will comprise much the same kind of food and service as at any other non-private dinner party.

What does change are the props. Windsor Castle has the finest collection in the world of rare old Waterford glass. It was all bought by George III and George IV and the glasses go off at an odd angle because each one is hand-made. This glass is used at a Dine and Sleep dinner party, and the footmen wear their scarlet jacket, black trousers, white tie and waistcoat. The pages wear white tie, stiff shirt and black coat, all with the gold EIIR buttons of the Queen.

Windsor Castle also has a surprising collection of chamber pots, though the Queen does not show these to her guests. They are kept in a cupboard in a small gothic, mirrored passage, between the State

Dining Room and the Octagonal Dining Room. They were always kept between the two dining rooms, as the nearest lavatory was a considerable distance away in Queen Victoria's day. In those days of gargantuan eating and drinking, they were there for the gentlemen guests' benefit. Happily for the staff, Windsor Castle now has a cloakroom, but the dozen or so chamber pots remain. And very pretty they are too.

The best part of Dine and Sleep as far as the guests are concerned is that dinner is always followed by a tour of the Windsor Castle library. This really is a rare privilege, as it is a room full of treasures that few people ever see. The Queen herself is fascinated by all that the room contains. It holds her family history, plus a fine collection of Leonardo da Vinci drawings. The Queen is very knowledgeable about what's what in the house, so at about ten-thirty she herself shows her guests around, and she is a fascinating guide. For members of the Household and the family, who know it all backwards, a temporary bar is set up with a vast array of drinks.

Of course, at various times throughout the totally predictable royal year the Queen is host to an official dinner – usually for around sixty people and held at Buckingham Palace. These dinners are more for politicians than for heads of state. The latter get the much grander state banquet, which is held in the Ballroom – a huge, high-ceilinged, cream-painted room with mouldings and pillars picked out in gold leaf, dominated by chandeliers and the Queen's thrones, set under a vast red velvet canopy. On these occasions, all of Queen Victoria's solid gold plate is brought out for the night.

The routine for a state banquet is like a well-rehearsed play, with curtain up at ten to eight on a spring or autumn Tuesday evening when Prince Philip leaves his and the Queen's apartments in Buckingham Palace. He runs downstairs in white tie and tails, ignoring the lift, to the Belgium Suite where the distinguished guests are waiting.

It might be the President of somewhere as important as the USA and his lady, or the head of state of any small foreign power. It could be foreign royalty, but no matter how rich or poor their country they are about to be treated to one of the greatest pieces of theatre that exists today, and it is all in their honour. Prince Philip is to escort them to the White Drawing Room, where most of the Royal Family are waiting to receive their guests. Drinks are served before the family go in procession to the Palace Ballroom for the banquet. It is considerably more impressive than simply taking dinner with the Queen – an experience that even the wealthiest and the most sophisticated of statesmen will never forget.

Once the guests have been taken to the White Drawing Room they are treated to a spectacular surprise that few ever see. Suddenly the fireplace and huge mirror that dominate the white and gold room swing back. Through this secret entrance the Queen enters from her own apartments, glittering in evening dress, tiara and priceless jewels. Then the fireplace swings back into place. And the state banquet, jewel in the crown of a state visit, can now begin.

Meanwhile that morning, deep in the basement of the Palace, safes will have been opened and Queen Victoria's gold plate washed in warm soapy water by the Yeoman of the Glass and China Pantry and his staff. The table will have been set with this gold plate and crystal glasses, and candelabra will have been placed dead centre down the long tables by the smallest and lighest footman. Wearing something like airline socks on his feet, he will have made his way down the middle of the table, making sure that each candelabra is absolutely symmetrical.

Just before the dinner begins, hundreds of ivory-coloured candles are lit, brilliantly illuminating the Ballroom. One hundred and sixty people will be seated, including high-ranking military men, church dignitaries and others with a special interest in the guest's country. Orders, miniatures and decorations are worn, and the women wear tiaras, long gloves and spectacular jewellery.

The Royal Family go in procession to the Ballroom, led by the Lord High Steward and the Lord Chamberlain carrying their wands of office. These two dignitaries have to walk backwards, facing the Queen and her guests, and there have been some tense moments over the years. The Queen partners the visiting head of state, while Prince Philip leads in the head of state's wife. Others follow in order of seniority.

This is one of the occasions when the Queen does not lead everyone in to dinner. All except the principal guests are assembled and waiting, standing by their little gilt chairs. Not until she is seated do they sit. Although the Archbishop of Canterbury is always present, grace is not said, in deference to the different religions of the many nationalities gathered together.

Above, in a small gallery, a regimental string orchestra plays softly, while dinner – invariably soup, lamb, pudding, fruit and petits fours – is served with military precision, facilitated by a 'traffic light' system between the kitchens and the banqueting room. Microphones are put in front of the Queen and the visiting head of state, ready for their speeches. Staff and their families are allowed to watch it all from behind a grille above the orchestra.

The Queen and her guests drink to the health of each other's country. Two hours have passed, and it is time for the Queen to lead the visitors into the drawing room for coffee . . . much to the relief of those who are dying for a cigarette or desperate to speak to someone in their own language. A state dinner can be quite a strain.

Here are some of the dishes served at royal dinners:

KIPPER SOUFFLÉ

SCAMPI MORNAY

SALMON QUICHE

PHEASANT NORMANDE

GLENFIDDICH CHOCOLATE MOUSSE

CARDINAL PEARS

KIPPER SOUFFLÉ

The Queen has loved kippers since she was a child and enjoys them at breakfast, as a savoury or even as a late-night snack. When she moved to Buckingham Palace shortly after her coronation, one of the first things she did was to place an order for a weekly box during the season.

8 oz (250 g) cooked kipper meat, flaked
1 tablespoon chopped parsley
1 oz (25 g) butter
1 tablespoon plain flour
¼ pint (150 ml) milk
Salt and pepper
3 eggs, separated
Lemon twists and parsley sprigs for garnish

Pre-heat the oven to 190°C/375°F/gas mark 5. Mash or pound the kippers in a pestle and mortar to a fine paste with the finely chopped parsley. Melt the butter over a low heat. Stir in the flour to make a roux, and cook until lightly browned. Add the milk a little at a time, beating well after each addition. Season to taste, remembering that the kippers themselves will be quite salty. Simmer gently for a few minutes, stirring, to cook the flour and until the sauce is creamy. Remove the pan from the heat and stir in the kipper paste. Beat in the egg yolks one at a time. Whip the egg whites until stiff and fold them into the mixture quickly. Turn into a 1½ pint (900 ml) buttered soufflé dish and bake for 20–30 minutes until browned. Serve garnished with lemon twists and parsley sprigs.

SCAMPI MORNAY

1 lb (450 g) scampi, fresh or frozen
A little seasoned flour
3 oz (90 g) butter
4 oz (125 g) button mushrooms, sliced
1 oz (25 g) plain flour
1 pint (600 ml) milk
1 teaspoon mustard powder
Salt and pepper
1 lb (450 g) cold mashed potato
2 oz (60 g) fresh breadcrumbs
4 oz (125 g) Cheddar cheese, grated
Parsley for garnish

Toss the scampi in the seasoned flour and fry in 2 oz (60 g) of the butter for 5 minutes. Remove and drain. Put the mushrooms in the same pan and fry gently until soft. In a separate pan melt the remaining 1 oz (25 g) of butter, stir in the flour to make a roux and cook gently until just beginning to brown. Add the milk a little at a time, stirring well to prevent sticking. Simmer gently for 5 minutes. Add the mustard powder and the seasoning. Take off the heat, and mix into the pan the scampi and the mushrooms, with any of the remaining juices. Fill a piping bag with the mashed potato and pipe around the edge of individual serving dishes. Spoon the scampi mixture into the centre. Mix the breadcrumbs and grated cheese together and sprinkle over the top. Brown under a hot grill or in a hot oven. Serve garnished with parsley.

SALMON QUICHE

Fresh salmon from the River Dee at Balmoral is renowned the world over. The Queen Mother in particular is a dab hand with the rod and line.

6 oz (175 g) shortcrust pastry
2 eggs plus one yolk
2 oz (60 g) Cheddar cheese, grated
Salt and black pepper
¼ pint (150 ml) single cream
2 oz (60 g) onion, finely sliced
1 oz (25 g) butter
4 oz (125 g) cold cooked salmon

Pre-heat the oven to 180°C/350°F/gas mark 4. Line a greased 8-inch (20-cm) flan dish with the pastry. Beat the eggs and cheese together and add the salt, pepper and cream. Sauté the onions in the butter until starting to change colour, add the salmon and cook, stirring gently, for a few minutes. Combine the salmon and cream mixtures and pour into the pastry case. Bake until golden brown. Serve hot or cold.

PHEASANT NORMANDE

4 oz (125 g) fat bacon rashers
1 large pheasant
2 oz (60 g) butter, melted
1 lb (450 g) cooking apples
4 oz (125 g) mushrooms, sliced
Salt and pepper
¼ pint (5 fl oz) single cream
1 tablespoon Calvados (optional)

Pre-heat the oven to 180°C/350°F/gas mark 4. Tie the bacon around the pheasant and brown it in a large pan with the melted butter. Peel, core and thickly slice the apples. Place the pheasant in a deep casserole dish and layer the apples and the mushrooms around it. Dribble with any remaining butter and season to taste. Mix the cream with the Calvados and pour over the pheasant. Cover and cook for about 1 hour, basting the bird occasionally with the juices.

GLENFIDDICH CHOCOLATE MOUSSE

6 oz (175 g) plain chocolate
4 eggs, separated
1 teaspoon vanilla essence
Grated rind of 1 orange
½ pint (300 ml) double cream
2 tablespoons Glenfiddich whisky
A little grated chocolate to garnish

Melt the chocolate over a pan of simmering water. Remove from the heat, cool, and beat in the egg yolks one at a time. Flavour with the vanilla essence and orange rind. Whip the cream until thick, stir in the whisky and fold this mixture into the chocolate. Beat the egg whites until stiff and fold them in carefully. Pour into one large dish or several individual dishes and chill for at least 2 hours. Sprinkle with a little grated chocolate before serving.

CARDINAL PEARS

6 oz (175 g) caster sugar
1 pint (600 ml) water
Strip of lemon peel
4 dessert pears
1 lb (450 g) raspberries
Icing sugar to taste
1 tablespoon Kirsch
2 tablespoons toasted flaked almonds

Dissolve the sugar and water over a low heat in a shallow pan to make a thin syrup. Add the lemon peel. Peel, core and halve the pears and place them flat side down in the syrup. Simmer until tender, cool, drain and place in a glass serving dish. Make the sauce by sieving the raspberries and mixing them with enough sugar to sweeten and the Kirsch. Pour the raspberry sauce over the pears and chill. Just before serving scatter with the toasted almonds.

9

A ROYAL WEDDING

All the world loves a wedding, and nothing fires the imagination of the British quite as much as a royal wedding. The day is an excuse for pageantry. Hundreds of thousands of well-wishers throng the capital to line the route of the procession, on an occasion which adds a great splash of glamour to daily life and a lot of excitement.

In some ways it's more fun for us than for the couple concerned. Unfortunately they aren't allowed too much say in their wedding. From the moment that their engagement is officially announced the royal machine takes over. Royal brides-to-be, like Lady Diana Spencer and Sarah Ferguson, more or less have to do what they are told. It's not just their wedding. It's a state occasion. It's not their day. It's a day for the people.

There are many differences between a royal wedding and an ordinary one, besides the scale of the event. Traditionally it is the bride's father who pays when his daughter marries, but when one of the royal princes weds the Queen picks up the bill regardless. This might well be a relief for the bride's family, considering how grand the wedding has to be. The snag is that the bride is not allowed to invite too many guests to the ceremony. Her family and friends may well be thin on the ground as she walks up the aisle.

The reason for this apparent injustice is that so many people are begging for invitations. The most important group of invitees are those known as the Magic Four Hundred. These consist of royalty from all over Europe who must be invited, regardless of whether they are still throned or long deposed. Not one single relative of the Queen must be left out. And, of course, there are the Queen's personal friends – those who make up her intimate circle.

Then there are a great many places requested by the Foreign Office 'for diplomatic reasons'. Presidents and heads of state of friendly countries are invited, along with their ambassadors. Representatives from the British government, the Church, the trade unions and the services must also be asked, and old family retainers are invited, including some of the staff from the Queen's private homes.

At Prince Charles's wedding, St Paul's Cathedral could have been filled four times over, but since space is always at a premium the happy couple have no choice but to accept a list largely consisting of people they have never met and will probably never meet again. Lady Diana and Sarah Ferguson didn't even have much influence on what was served at the wedding breakfast. The menu for the day is decided by the Queen, and she usually settles for a cold buffet of lobster, salmon, chicken and tiny lamb cutlets accompanied by various salads.

One consolation, however, is that at least the royal bride-to-be does not have to bear the burden of sending out the thousands of gold-edged invitation cards. They are always from the Queen. Nor does she have to worry about cars and transport for everyone. All this is done by the tireless Lord Chamberlain and his staff. He also masterminds the procession and the troops to line the route. He arranges every detail of the venue, and this, of course, is the first of the many important decisions that are made. The usual location chosen is Westminster Abbey, since it's near the Palace. Occasionally St Paul's is an alternative on a royal occasion because the fine old Wren cathedral seats more people – as was necessary when Prince Charles and Lady Diana married.

Lady Diana was not particularly enamoured with these workings of the royal machine, and grumbled at how little say she had in her own wedding. No doubt Sarah Ferguson felt the same. But their wishes took second place to the royal arrangements – just as the wishes of the bride whom Prince Edward finally chooses will be.

Of course, although press speculation will be endless and the Palace will blandly deny any such thing as a romance, there's no great gasp of surprise in royal circles when an engagement is finally announced. By the time the Royal Family are ready to go public with the news, they are very certain that the newcomer will fit in. The bride- (or groom-) to-be has already been received into the bosom of this very close-knit 'firm' as Prince Philip calls the Royal Family.

As soon as the announcement is made, congratulatory telegrams begin arriving by the thousands and flowers by the vanful. They pour in from all over the world. Most of the flowers are immediately sent to old folks' homes and hospitals. If they weren't, the Palace would be like an oversized flower shop. There is no great interval between the engagement and wedding, as saving for a mortgage is not an issue for a royal couple. Between four and five months after the engagement ring is slipped on the finger, the marriage band follows.

Similarly, there are no great problems about fixing a date, though again this is chosen by the machine. There is always plenty of time and forewarning to ensure that everything runs smoothly. All royal fixtures, including weddings, are plotted six months in advance. When a romance looks like becoming serious, long before an engagement is announced, the Palace officials who plan the royal routine block off a space in the royal diary in anticipation. Spontaneity is not something the Royal Family ever indulge in. Though the Prince of Wales announced his engagement at the end of January, he had known for some months that he intended to propose – it must have required great strength of mind to keep it to himself. Had Lady Diana done the unthinkable and turned him down, the Prince would have had a lot of time for polo in the summer of 1981.

But, of course, she said yes. The Lord Chamberlain's office was therefore able to get on with the seating arrangements for the cathedral. These are most certainly not on a first-come-first-served basis. The seating plan is a miracle of organization, with every wedding guest given their own seat number. And there are many gentlemen ushers in attendance to make sure everyone is in their right place.

Different areas in the abbey or cathedral are delineated by strictly colour-coded numbers. This prevents the sort of embarrassing situation where a gamekeeper who arrives early is put in a front seat while a duchess who arrives later gets tucked in at the back. It's a delicate business ensuring that no one is offended. People noticed that, at Prince Charles's wedding, Nancy Reagan was stuck behind the King of Tonga. Odd, they thought. But by royal reckoning, if you're a king, even of the tiniest country in the world, you're more important than a president's wife.

As a rule, at ordinary weddings everyone who goes to the church goes to the wedding breakfast or lunch. This is another tradition which is turned round at a royal wedding. The guest list for the festivities back at the Palace is a small one, probably comprising no more than forty guests, only the select few and immediate family.

For those who might otherwise feel themselves left out in the cold, the Queen gives a ball two nights before the wedding. As many of the Magic Four Hundred as can be squeezed in are asked. The bride's side is probably allowed about a hundred places at this most glittering affair, which does at least mop up those friends and family who have not managed to get invited to the wedding ceremony. But an awful lot of editing of the list is inevitable, and there are still those who cannot be included.

Major Ronald Ferguson decided to give a dance for his daughter three nights before the wedding, so most of her extensive circle of friends could be included in part of the celebrations, if not at the wedding itself. A large tented area in the polo ground at Smith's Lawn, Windsor, was the venue for 750 guests. Almost all the Royal Family were there, as was Nancy Reagan, who had flown from the USA for the wedding itself. The Major and his attractive wife, Sue, hosted the party, which consisted of a dinner for the immediate Royal Family first and then a dance with breakfast for Fergie and Andrew's friends. Apart from the pouring rain, the evening was a great success.

One tradition common to both ordinary and royal weddings is the stag night. But the royal variation is generally held some days before the wedding, to prevent having a hungover bridegroom on the wedding morning. Fergie and Diana decided to intrude on Prince Andrew's stag night. They dressed themselves up as policewomen and took themselves off to Annabel's, the exclusive Mayfair night-club, where they thought the stag night was taking place in a private room. A couple of friends saw through the disguises, however, and they were forced to leave, after much giggling, only to accost Andrew later at the gates of Buckingham Palace. Fergie, still in her police-woman's uniform, tried to prevent him from entering. Andrew, who enjoys outwitting everyone, had changed the stag night venue several times. But he was not expecting to be stopped at the gates of his home by a policewoman who bore a suspicious resemblance to his wife-to-be!

Once the wedding is over and the new husband and wife are safely back at the Palace, the official photographer waits in the room behind the Palace balcony to record the event for posterity. The balcony appearances and photography create a convenient time gap for the other guests to get back to the Palace through the crowded streets of rejoicing spectators.

Between one-thirty and two pm the favoured guests sit down behind the closed doors of the chosen reception room – usually the magnificent Bow Room after drinks in the 1844 Room next door. While the Bow Room is big enough to accommodate all the immediate royals, the foreign branches of the family usually go off to eat at their own embassies. There's not even enough room for the parents of some of the bridesmaids and pages. They eat their lunch in the Household dining room, alongside members of the Household.

The attendant footmen are always left outside the firmly closed Bow Room doors, only appearing when rung for. Inside the sanctuary the Royal Family and their guests eat their cold buffet, make the congratulatory toasts and cut the cake – with a sword – which often leads to a lot of good-natured noise and giggles.

The ceremonial cake is always made by the Palace chefs, but there is friendly rivalry from the catering corps of the three armed services, who each make a cake of their own. They compete to create the most splendid and mouth-watering cake of all to outdo the culinary skills of the Palace chef. There are also a considerable number of amazingly professional-looking cakes that arrive from the public as presents. These are all put on display and eventually cut up, neatly boxed and distributed to staff and to friends who weren't at the wedding.

All the arrangements have to run with split-second precision, and this means a very busy time for the Queen's staff. From the moment that the announcement of the engagement is made, all staff leave is cancelled until after the wedding, but no one minds. Everyone who works at the Palace wants to be involved in the action and excitement and to know exactly what's going on.

The Palace has its own very efficient grapevine, and more often than not the staff knows what's happening days before the announcement is made in the Court Circular. But once the news is confirmed the Master of the Household puts in a request for the staff's drinks issue, which reminds the Queen of an old Palace tradition.

She instantly says yes and personally gives the order to the Yeoman of the Cellar, either through her intercom system, or perhaps through one of her boxes (Palace memos) if there is time. Then everyone can splice the mainbrace – the Royal Navy's historic term for a celebratory issue of rum – and drink the royal health. The cellarmen work overtime to quench the staff's thirst, and literally hundreds of bottles of wine are distributed throughout the Palace.

Stewards' room and upwards get champagne. Staff get wine. The kitchen are served separately. Lots of people get a bit tipsy, since the allowance is a generous one and there is a marvellous atmosphere of heady celebration throughout the Palace. The staff immediately start a collection for the wedding present: depending on the level of job, contributions range from 50p to £2. Prince Charles's staff bought him silver menu holders fashioned in the shape of the Prince of Wales feathers. These were welcome, since no royal meal is served without menu cards. Then comes the lull before the storm. The officials are busy dealing with the details of the wedding day, arranging the royal yacht for the honeymoon, and acknowledging telegrams, flowers and gifts. Until the actual day dawns, the staff have comparatively little to do. But when it does come, it's all hands on deck with the normal routine out of kilter.

The Palace becomes even more of a well-oiled machine, and each valuable member one of its cogs. All day people are eating snatched meals in shifts, particularly in the staff dining room, where lunch is served at half-hour intervals to accommodate those who have been on carriage duty, or at the cathedral or abbey. Thus the senior staff have a very early lunch while the ceremony is going on, so that they are ready to go on duty at the door for the return of the wedding party. The stable men, on the other hand, don't get lunch until about four o'clock – all the horses have to have their harness taken off and be stabled, and the carriages have to be put away. The footmen who have been riding pillion on the carriages are ready for their meal and a glass of wine or champagne to drink the royal toast much earlier.

Inevitably it is the kitchens that are the most overworked areas of the bustling Palace, coping with all the preparations for and serving of the wedding breakfast, while trying at the same time to keep the rest of the Palace fed at such varying times. An event as major as a royal wedding necessitates the drafting in of extra staff. It would be far too much to expect the regulars to cope with all the added preparations. Once they are kitted out in their livery, dating from Queen Victoria's time, no one would be able to tell the difference between them and the old hands. Since these casual workers have to be paid more than Palace staff – about what ordinary staff get for two or three days' work – to keep the peace the Queen gives her regulars overtime and a bonus.

Then around three-thirty the stables are busy again, with more carriages being prepared for the royal couple's departure at four o'clock. Upstairs, the honeymooners are changing into their going away clothes, ready for departure – but to where? That's just what the world's press are clamouring to know, and although the venue of the first night of the honeymoon is always a well-kept secret, the couple are usually treated to a cruise – Princess Anne and Mark Phillips went to the West Indies, Charles and Diana chose the Mediterranean, and Fergie and Andrew the Azores. Privacy is at a premium for royalty and no press launch, however persistent, has yet been able to follow *Britannia* on her secret honeymoon routes.

Just like all marriages, royal weddings have their memories. . . . Princess Diana muddled her husband's names during the service. Sarah repeated Andrew's name twice in her anxiety not to make a mistake. It was Prince William who, as one of the sailor-suited page boys, stole the show at her wedding. Few people who watched the service will ever forget his wriggling and jiggling. He was seated next to his cousin, Laura Fellowes, and halfway through the service began to get bored. He fiddled with the cord of his sailor hat, pushing it to the back of his head. He then tried to remove the mini knife that was part of his outfit. Having failed, he tried to engage the attention of Laura Fellowes. She refused to be distracted, so he stuck his tongue out at her. The television crews, who had been asked not to focus too much of their attention on the group of bridesmaids and pages, did their best to keep the cameras on the business in hand, but could not resist the occasional close-up of William's antics.

When the Royal Family reminisce about previous weddings, Princess Alexandra's to Angus Ogilvy is always mentioned even though it was long ago. It was perhaps the nearest to a real family wedding that it is possible for the royals to have, and Princess Alexandra herself is the most popular member within the royal circle, loved by everyone. Her pre-wedding party was held at Windsor and was very grand, but the royals still remember it as the best ever.

It's a family joke remembering how Prince Charles upset the make-up artist on the day of Princess Anne's wedding. The Queen had left her own rooms and gone upstairs, as the mother of the bride, to see how her daughter was. A French cosmetic artist had just finished making up Princess Anne's face, and Charles, who was with his mother, said: 'Oh, Anne, you've got far too much make-up on.'

The French make-up artist bridled and said crossly: 'Perhaps His Highness would like some as well?'

'No thanks,' said Charles and, eyebrows raised, fled back down the corridor.

There was a time when to be royal meant marrying for duty. The Queen's grandmother, the stately Queen Mary, had originally been engaged to the Duke of Clarence. His death changed the situation. But Queen Victoria, convinced that Mary of Teck would make good royal stock, was determined that she should marry *one* of the royal princes. Dutifully, Mary married her dead fiancé's brother, and became Queen when he ascended the throne as King George V.

No one would be expected to make such a sacrifice today, and indeed, within reason, royalty today can marry whom they like. Though the union of Prince Andrew with actress Koo Stark was vetoed by Prince Philip, the last ten years have seen two men of the Royal Family – Prince Michael of Kent and the Earl of St Andrews – marrying women who were both divorced and Catholic, something that would have been unthinkable twenty years ago.

Even the Queen, who fell deeply in love with Prince Philip while she was just fifteen, had her problems. Her father, King George VI, was not certain that the British public would take a Greek prince of German descent to their hearts. The fact that Prince Philip had fought in the Royal Navy during the war and spent most of his life in Britain did not ease the King's reluctance. It was only the young Princess's determination – with a little help from the late Lord Louis Mountbatten, Prince Philip's uncle – to marry the man she loved that eventually brought into being one of this century's most successful marriages.

It was a wedding that took place in the aftermath of war, when Britain was deep into austerity. At first it was going to be held quietly and privately in St George's Chapel at Windsor, but then the Labour government of the day relented and permitted the marriage to become a public occasion, realizing that such a festivity could only lift the hearts of a war-weary people. And the people showed astonishing generosity when the news was announced. Women sent sugar and flour from their meagre rations to help towards the wedding cake; others sent the young Princess Elizabeth precious nylon stockings and hoarded lengths of fabric for her gown. People even sent books of their clothing coupons, but these had to be returned since it was illegal for them to be passed on.

Nothing changes. When royalty marries, in spite of their wealth and riches, the gifts still pour in. There were so many at Charles and Diana's wedding that the Queen turned what was called the old Tradesmen's Entrance at Buckingham Palace into the Side Gate, changing the name so as not to offend people who sent presents.

While most people use initiative and inspiration when choosing gifts that they think the royal couple concerned might like, governments ask advice. The Canadian government presented Charles and Diana with an entire bedroom suite, including wardrobes, dressing tables and a four-poster bed, all in Canadian maple. In these cases royalty aren't backward in coming forward about saying what they would like!

Both Diana and Fergie left their wedding lists with the General Trading Company in Sloane Street, in London, an ideal situation which should have ensured that only wanted presents would be bought for them. But this wasn't so. No one sent Diana a toaster – she had to buy one – and the Royals are as bedevilled with terrible wedding presents as any other couple. The worst present that Prince Charles received is said to have come from an elderly duke. It was a sort of mobile cloakroom: a coat rail with a red plastic cover, with hooks attached for each coat. The idea seemed to be for security, as every coat hung on it could be chained into place. Looking like a wardrobe chopped in half, it is said to be absolutely hideous and was last seen languishing in the billiard room at Highgrove, gathering dust.

But then it's the thought that counts, isn't it?

Royal holidays are usually spent at Sandringham in Norfolk or Balmoral in Scotland. Here Fergie follows the shoot with her gun dog, Tarn. Her Christmas pudding hat was made for her by a friend, Marina Killery.

The Queen Mother walking on the Sandringham beach with her two corgis, Ranger and Dash. The Duchess of Grafton, the Queen's Mistress of the Robes (senior Lady-in-Waiting) is with her.

In royal households, everything stops for tea and even when travelling, the Queen loves nothing better than her afternoon cuppa.

Every milk bottle bears the royal cipher and the milk is delivered to Buckingham Palace from the Windsor dairy herd. At table, milk is always served in a silver jug.

The Queen always tries
to follow the customs of
the country. Here, with
some trepidation, she
joins her host King
Hassan of Morocco as
he eats with his
hands from the banquet
of lamb.

All the glamour of a state
banquet at Windsor
Castle, captured by a
photographer high on a
balcony, who is not
allowed the benefit of
flash photography. The
Queen leads the royal
party into dinner
followed by the Queen
Mother, the Dean of
Windsor, the Princess of
Wales and Prince Philip.

Travelling in canine style: one of the royal corgis gets a helping hand from a crew member as they leave after a visit to Scotland on board an aircraft of the Queen's Flight.

The odd assortment of royal luggage on the quayside waiting to be loaded on to the royal yacht, Britannia, belongs to the Queen and her party. Different coloured labels (The Queen uses yellow) are used for various royal family members.

Footmen in livery of scarlet jacket and black breeches. Until recently they were chosen in pairs, to be of matching heights when riding on the carriages. Here they drive the Queen Mother, her great grandson, Prince William, and The Princess of Wales to the Trooping the Colour ceremony at Horseguards Parade from Buckingham Palace.

The Queen Mother's beloved page, William, in his black-trousered livery complete with medals, which both pages (the higher rank) and footmen wear if they are entitled to do so. William is accompanying Viscount Linley down the drive of Clarence House on his grandmother, the Queen Mother's birthday.

For the daytime, Diana opts for the preppy look, complete with a boyish tie and tailored shirt.

An emerald green silk waistcoat from the men's shop, Hacketts, completes Diana's evening look. Her tuxedo and wing-collared shirt is so smart, it would put most men to shame.

The Princess with her model-girl figure looks as stunning in masculine
clothing as she does in a ball gown. Tight jeans, cowboy boots and a baseball
cap complete Diana's American look.

The Queen and the Queen Mother chatting outside the church at Windsor on Christmas morning.

Being Queen doesn't mean that receiving presents isn't fun. At Christmas the Royal Family open all their gifts on Christmas Eve. Carefully arranged on long tressle tables, each member of the family has their own pile of gifts, with the smaller things under the tree.

10

SUPPER WITH ROYALTY

When the Queen is attending a royal film premiere, a theatre command performance, or perhaps a very rare private evening at the ballet or opera, she and her guests always eat a light snack at about seven-fifteen before leaving home. The Queen and her guests congregate, in all their finery, upstairs in her private dining room at Buckingham Palace. Usually the party consists of the Duke, Prince Charles and Princess Diana, along with the Duke and Duchess of York if they are at home and Prince Edward. On some occasions the Queen Mother and Princess Margaret will also be present.

If it is an official royal 'do', the tradition is that everyone leaves from Buckingham Palace in one party, though probably in several cars. The Royal Family, whose whole life revolves around meals, take this little early supper snack to sustain them through the evening. Years of experience have taught them that royal galas have a habit of running overtime, and hunger pangs can set in. Once the performance is finally over, they get back home for real supper. The custom is for every member of the group to start and finish the evening at the Palace.

Real supper varies; the little light snack never does. It is always a big dish of scrambled eggs on a silver salver and another of smoked salmon, both carried in by the duty footman. A light German white wine accompanies it. The egg dish is placed on a hotplate on the sideboard, the salmon nearby but away from the heat. The brown bread is already buttered and cut into triangles, set on a plate. Plates, napkins and forks have been placed on the sideboard. The footman then disappears, and the Royal Family take a plate and fork, and serve themselves. They don't sit down formally, but drape themselves around the room, either on chairs or standing up and chatting.

They only eat a tiny amount of these pre-theatre refreshments, as they call them. No pudding follows. Then they leave for their function, returning to the Palace usually around half-past ten for the last meal of the day – proper late supper.

This meal will be laid and ready in the private dining room by the time their Rolls-Royces drive back into the Palace through the Garden Entrance. The food is deliberately cold in case the performance does go over the allotted time. They will eat chicken in aspic, or maybe cold lamb cutlets, cold salmon, cold mixed meats and salads followed by fresh fruit salad. Before they arrive, the food is set out where the hotplates stand so that they can help themselves before settling down around the table.

Again the wine will be their favourite German hock, though they drink – and eat – modestly at this late hour. The Queen likes those members of the Household who have been in attendance at the performance to join the supper party when they get back. The equerries and ladies-in-waiting who have merely been working late at the Palace eat in their own Household dining room.

When supper is over, the Queen's family, none of them night birds except for the Queen Mother and Princess Margaret, make their way back to the Garden Entrance where their cars will be waiting to take them to their own various residences. The Queen says 'Goodnight' from the top of her own stairs to the Garden Entrance, and a page or footman escorts her guests to their car. The Night Sergeant (the duty policeman who guards the Queen's bedroom, sitting in a little cubby-hole outside in the corridor), is sent for, and the Queen and the Duke go to bed. So do the staff, with a sigh of relief.

The Queen Mother is more of a late-night party giver, and she likes to take a group of her friends to a theatre. An evening in her company will always be varied. Guests are invited first to Clarence House for a little light snack – exactly as at Buckingham Palace. The difference is in the menu. The Queen Mother gives her guests a wide choice of really delicious canapés: things like asparagus wrapped in brown bread, and plates of assorted delicate little sandwiches. She follows the same pattern as her daughter in that everyone comes for these snacks and drinks in her morning room before going to the show. The other difference is that, while the Queen serves only white wine, the Queen Mother offers a wide range of drinks, already mixed and handed by her footman from a salver.

The Queen Mother has much grander after-theatre suppers and always serves hot food. If she goes to a film premiere she takes about fourteen guests and asks them all back to Clarence House. She also invites her Household to the party: no one is ever left out. The dining table will be laid up while Her Majesty is at the theatre, and there is no question of her guests helping themselves. A full staff will be on duty to serve and clear. These gatherings go on much longer than the Queen's. It's usual to sit down at about midnight at Clarence House, and people don't leave until the early hours – the Queen Mother is not mad about going to bed. The staff might be tired out, but she is still full of beans and quite happy for the evening to go on. She appears inexhaustible.

The Queen Mother likes slightly richer food than her chef approves of, and he has a rather boring habit of marking with a star what he thinks is his dish of the day when he presents her with her menu book. She never takes any notice, and her guests are likely to be served one of her out-of-season 'little treats' – her own pet way of describing something wildly expensive. So in December the meal might consist of asparagus, lobster and strawberries.

She is a very precise party planner. Her duty staff – and there are usually around ten of them – are told at least a week before how many there will be for supper. Royal style is rarely spontaneous – everything has to be planned ahead, and an extra guest is highly unlikely to be unexpectedly invited.

When the Royal Family attend the opera or the ballet at Covent Garden, the routine is totally different: they take their own supper with them. And on the nights when royalty are occupying the Royal Box, the people in the audience who stare up at them rarely realize exactly what is going on behind the scenes.

What few people know – and they can't see from the auditorium – is that behind the Royal Box there is a private dining room. The Royal Family slip through a door from the box into this tall, elegant, flower-filled room, which will easily seat a dozen for dinner. (The flowers are by courtesy of the Royal Opera House.) In the corner of the room a full bar will have been laid, this time provided by the

Palace staff, as it's cheaper to bring wine and spirits from the Palace cellars. There are times when they run out of wine and have to buy some from the Opera House, which always causes royal grumbles as it is much more expensive than raiding the Buckingham Palace cellars.

The Royal Box also contains a small private lavatory and wash-basin. The royal staff take fresh soap and towels from the Palace when any member of the family is occupying the box.

For an opera supper the food, silver and cutlery all leave the Palace at five-thirty in a Range Rover, or a car with a lot of room in the back. Everything must arrive a good two hours before the opera begins, and it's organized in much the same way as a shooting lunch. Plates, knives and forks, table linen and so on are taken with the food itself, packed on big wooden butlers' trays at the Palace. It is then ferried to the Royal Box entrance on the Floral Street side of the Opera House. Then the staff start working on the box's dining room so that by seven the table is laid with Palace silver, crystal and bone china. Later the car goes back to the Palace to collect a big container of ice for the wine and Prince Charles's favourite drink, the famous lemon refresher. Ice cream is also collected in a refrigerated container. Two footmen do the job, and it's hard work, involving a lot of humping up and down the Opera House staircases. When Alan Fisher was Prince Charles's butler, before he returned to the United States, he even took candelabra. He had great style, but even in the ordinary way menus are printed and everything is done in the grand manner.

It is a marvellous experience to be taken to the Opera House by one of the Royal Family. Sometimes they make up a really big party, using as an overspill the adjoining box which belongs to the British Council. Prince Charles is the family's greatest opera buff and uses the box more than anyone else. He usually has five guests accompanying him and he likes supper to coincide with the first interval.

One of his staff – usually the valet – has to find out the times of the intervals and instruct the footmen to be ready to serve the food at, say, ten minutes past eight. The valet, usually parked in the British Council box, has to keep an eye on his watch. Two minutes before the curtain goes up again he slips quietly into the Retiring Room and whispers: 'Two minutes, sir,' to the Prince. He then turns all the lights off in the Royal Box so that the Prince and his party can slide in without being seen.

All the food at Covent Garden is cold except when the hostess is the Queen Mother. She always prefers hot meals, and to keep the food hot her staff use shooting boxes of the same type as those used at Sandringham and Balmoral. These silver boxes, which contain an inner padded wooden box, were made back in Edward VII's time, though some have Queen Victoria's cipher, making them even older. They keep food remarkably hot.

The Queen and Prince Philip prefer cold food because it's easier to manage – particularly in the mad scramble to get through a course, served by the footmen in their day livery, before the end of the interval. The usual choice is cold chicken curry, a dish they all enjoy. They will have a starter – perhaps a little egg drum kilbo – if there is time. Normally they try to eat the first and main course in the first interval; pudding and coffee in the second. If they're running late, they leave their plates on the table with food on them, go back to watch the opera, and then just come back and continue eating at the next opportunity. If there are only two short intervals, there's always a rush to have their coffee before going back in. After curtain-up the footmen madly clear the dining room, as it must be perfect, with no trace of the meal, when the Royal Family come back through.

Sometimes in the intervals, if one of Prince Charles's favourites, like Kiri Te Kanawa or Placido Domingo is performing, he receives them in the box during the second interval. They pop upstairs quickly by the backstage stairs in all their make-up and robes. These are the occasions when the wine runs out!

What is interesting is that the Queen can't stand the opera and only ever goes on gala nights. Charles loves it, while Diana is lukewarm, preferring the ballet, to which she usually takes her sister. The Duke and Duchess of Kent are passionate about grand opera, and use the Royal Box as much as they can. When they go, the Opera House does the catering – usually something simple like salmon – and sends a bill later. If the Royal Family aren't using the box, sometimes the Covent Garden manager will put a VIP in, with the permission of the Royal Family.

It is only on special occasions that the Royal Family eat supper. It is not a meal to which they ever sit down in private – in other words, when they are alone. Yet astonishingly, when there are house party guests at Balmoral and Sandringham, after the film has been shown they eat yet again, even though they have had an enormous dinner. Chicken sandwiches (with no crusts) are the usual choice, left by the footmen next to the drinks trays and eaten at around midnight.

The sandwiches are arranged on a silver dish, under silver lids, and actually rarely get eaten (hardly surprising). When they are left, they are a great treat for the duty staff who eat them with their bed-time mugs of tea. The Queen does not mind, as sandwiches will not keep.

Things are a little different at Highgrove, Prince Charles and Princess Diana's country home. They always have a light supper on Sundays, which they eat in front of the television. They go for scrambled eggs, eggs Florentine or quiches.

Stephen Barry, the Prince's valet who died so tragically of AIDS, said that he became a dab hand at eggs Florentine, with a variation. 'The Prince used to like leeks from his own garden, picked by his own royal hand, used as a base for the eggs and the spinach, and the cheese sauce always had to be double thickness.'

He talked, too, of a different kind of supper.

'One of the pleasures of working for the Prince that I remember with great affection were the suppers that we used to have on the train from Aberdeen to Euston,' he said. 'These were a fairly regular happening when the Prince had to come back to London after a brief fishing trip to Scotland. When he was travelling privately we would go by ordinary train, reserving four sleepers for our own use. We never booked in our real names. The Prince was always Mr Brown.

'The only way that the public might guess that something was up was that there were rather more railway police about than usual. And the train was cleaner and, amazingly, the heating seemed to work. My sleeping compartment would be to one side of the Prince, next to me the two railway police with both walkie-talkies and radios which used to keep me awake all night, and on the other side of him, his own policemen occupied the fourth compartment.

'We always took packed supper. I chose the menu and Chef made up the food and packed it in a big wicker picnic basket, with THE QUEEN written on it in brass. Life went on with style even in the train. I even carried the Prince's pre-dinner Martini mix in a tonic bottle, with ice in a travelling themos bucket.

'The food was usually salmon mayonnaise, cold lamb cutlets with mint jelly, cold chicken, selections of salads and a marvellous pudding, a great favourite called Sandringham orange. This is made from oranges sliced very thinly with the skin still on, and covered with syrup. All the food was under plastic lids, like Tupperware, and packed along with the ordinary, Kings pattern travelling silver and cruets. We had plastic plates and plastic beakers to drink from. We used tonic bottles with screw tops for the Prince's lemon refresher. We didn't bother with wine. It was my job to set it all out, and, meant in the nicest possible way, the left-overs went to the railway police. The chef used to pack as if we'd been marooned for a week, and the Prince knew there was no buffet or restaurant on the train. He wouldn't let anyone go hungry.

'When supper-time came, we would open the door between my compartment and the Prince's, and he'd sit on his bed while his detective and I sat on mine. Once I'd emptied it, we would use the hamper as a table, and the three of us would sit there enjoying our supper, while the train rattled on down to London. The Prince would have thought it silly to eat in solitary state.

'He would lock the doors of his compartment when he slept and generally everything went splendidly. Occasionally we'd get one or two guards trying to be clever, asking for his ticket, but it was my job to deal with that. The only other perk was that Harvey, the Royal Labrador, was allowed to sleep in with his master and therefore spared the guard's van.

'I would pack everything away in the basket after we had eaten, and then we would leave the basket in the care of the guard. A railway attendant would take it on the next train back to Scotland, which kept the baskets in Scotland where they belong. They started going missing for a while until we worked out this system. The Royal Family do not care for losing things.

'We also used to picnic on long night car journeys. The Prince liked to drive and the detective and I would take it in turns with him so we all managed to eat a snack, packed by the pantry in the same big wicker picnic basket, except this time we didn't bother too much with cutlery. Bacon sandwiches were top favourite, along with the Sandringham oranges as pudding, in spite of the fact that they slopped around a bit.'

From bacon sandwiches to elegant canapés. At one time, the Queen used to give one really grand supper, usually in November. Two thousand people, including all London's foreign ambassadors, their wives and staffs, were invited. Most of the government and high-ranking Foreign Office officials were present. This diplomatic reception still takes place, but the supper has been abandoned for canapés, and the champagne for an open bar, both on the grounds of economy.

It is still one of the most splendid nights of the year, when the Queen meets her guests in the long Picture Gallery at the Palace. The staff are in their state livery. The biggest standard the Royal Family possess is flying on the flagpole above the Palace, and the entire building is open and brilliantly lit, vast crystal chandeliers lighting up family portraits and blazing down on the polyglot collection of partygoers.

The two thousand guests begin to arrive in their chauffeur-driven Rolls-Royces and Mercedes at about nine, queuing down The Mall to get to the Palace. Everyone from third world countries wears national costume. There are Chinese in tunics, Nigerians in the most brilliant colours, Indians in turbans and Arabs in robes. Western guests are in white tie and tails, their wives in evening dress. All the men wear their medals, and some of the South American diplomats have rows and rows of them! The men of the Royal Family are in breeches and white tie, and wearing all their decorations and orders. The Queen herself and the royal ladies dress in spectacular evening gowns and tiaras, and wear all their orders, too.

The reception proper begins at about nine-thirty, when the Queen arrives in the Picture Gallery by way of huge mirrored doors. The trumpeters of the Household sound a fanfare to announce her presence, and the crowd parts to allow her passage. It is pre-arranged exactly whom she will meet. She moves slowly along the length of the Picture Gallery, and gentlemen ushers bring forward those who have been chosen. These are mostly new arrivals to the Court of St James, who will have been presented to her in the previous twelve months. She moves on through the East Gallery into the huge Ballroom, and then into the ball supper room where the main bars and food are.

All the time, accompanied by other members of the family, she is smiling, shaking hands and greeting people in several languages, mostly French. Being diplomats, the guests are very proper about court etiquette, and bow and curtsey to the manner born. The Queen will have 'gone back through', as the Royal Family call it, into her private apartment after about ninety minutes, but the party goes on and so do the traffic jams in the Mall.

The main function of the royal kitchen on this night of nights is to produce about twenty thousand canapés, and they will have been preparing them for several days. They are handed round on silver salvers by footmen and by extra staff brought in from the royal yacht and from Thanet Catering College. For once the chefs get a brief glimpse of what's going on. As the delicious canapés disappear down the throats of the distinguished guests, more and more are brought up from the kitchen. The chefs wheel them on trolleys to temporary hotplates behind screens in the ball supper room, and the footmen go to these trays for replenishments. Some food is also left on the bars, which are set up on long trestle tables covered with long white cloths. The drinks, which are already made up, are pretty weak – not out of meanness, but to help people stay sober. The late Labour politician, Lord George Brown, used to get magnificently smashed by dint of going back to the bar rather too often. This used to amuse the Royal Family, particularly Princess Margaret. They were all extremely fond of him, and the officials were instructed to watch him to make sure he didn't fall over.

The party finishes around midnight, but most people go when the Queen leaves or once their presence has been registered. The crush is so great it's truly not a comfortable party, though guests do enjoy seeing the inside of the Palace. When only the last stragglers are left, the Household gather in one of the drawing rooms with a bar to have a nightcap on their own and relax, talking the evening over like the rest of us do. The Queen will be back in her rooms, having had an early dinner before attending the reception. No doubt she kicks her shoes off and thinks to herself, 'Well, that's that for another year, thank heavens.'

Late-night suppers at the Palace might include:

MUSHROOMS À LA CRÊME

COLD POACHED EGGS WITH WATERCRESS SAUCE

SCOTCH WOODCOCK

SANDRINGHAM ORANGE

MUSHROOMS À LA CRÊME

Breakfast and supper snacks such as mushrooms à la crême are Prince Philip's speciality, and when he rustles up a dish it is certain to be done to perfection.

2 oz (60 g) butter
1 lb (450 g) white button mushrooms, sliced
2 oz (60 g) plain flour
½ pint (300 ml) milk
Grated nutmeg to taste
Salt and pepper
2 tablespoons single cream
Croûtons and parsley sprigs for garnish

Melt the butter over a low heat and gently soften the mushrooms. Sprinkle on the flour and stir until the butter has been absorbed. Add the milk a little at a time, stirring well. Season with the nutmeg and salt and pepper. Simmer for 5 minutes, stirring, until the sauce is thick and smooth. Stir in the cream, transfer to a heated serving dish, scatter with the croûtons and garnish with parsley sprigs.

COLD POACHED EGGS WITH WATERCRESS SAUCE

The Queen insists that brown eggs taste better, regardless of scientific evidence that there is no difference. Brown or white eggs can be used for the following recipe, but for true authenticity, follow Her Majesty's example!

8 large eggs plus 3 extra yolks

6 oz (175 g) watercress

Salt and black pepper

1 teaspoon mustard powder

1 clove garlic, crushed

½ pint (300 ml) olive or vegetable oil

1 tablespoon white wine vinegar

Poach the eggs in barely simmering water for 3 minutes. A teaspoon of vinegar added to the poaching water will help prevent the whites from breaking up. Lift the cooked eggs out, drain and place in a bowl of cold water. Wash and dry the watercress leaves. Remove the stalks, reserving a few for garnish. Break the extra egg yolks into a blender or a bowl and add the seasoning, mustard and garlic. Blend briefly. Dribble in the oil very slowly (if you are using a bowl, beat it in with a wooden spoon). Stop occasionally if the oil is not totally absorbed. Add the vinegar and the watercress leaves and blend or beat again. Drain the cold poached eggs and place them on a serving dish. Pour the sauce over them and garnish with the reserved watercress leaves.

SCOTCH WOODCOCK

Another of Prince Philip's savoury specialities.

6 anchovies, drained
1 oz (25 g) butter, softened
Black pepper to taste
4 slices thin white bread
3 egg yolks
½ pint (300 ml) single cream

Pound the anchovies with the butter and black pepper. Toast the bread and spread with the anchovy paste. Beat the egg yolks and cream together, then place in a saucepan on a low heat. Cook until creamy, stirring continually. Cut the toast into triangles, top with the scrambled egg and serve piping hot.

SANDRINGHAM ORANGE

At state banquets or receptions, the Queen will often ask for a glass of fresh orange juice. Here is a simple orange pudding which retains all the fresh orange taste that can be lost in more elaborate recipes.

1½ pints (900 ml) fresh orange juice
2 oz (60 g) ground rice
1 orange
2 oz (60 g) granulated sugar

Heat the orange juice and ground rice over a low heat, stirring until it thickens. Grate the rind from the orange and add to the pan with the sugar. Bring to the boil and simmer until the sugar is dissolved. Pour into glass dishes and decorate with orange slices with all the white pith removed. Serve cold.

11

ROYAL CELEBRATIONS

In the coming years, the biggest of all royal celebrations will be changing its venue. Instead of the Royal Family going to Windsor Castle for the Christmas get-together, the Queen, Prince Philip and their family will go instead to Sandringham. The reason is a practical one. At the time of writing, one of the largest surviving castles in Europe is being repaired and refurbished and will not be habitable – apart from a few rooms – until at least 1990.

It means the return to an old routine. Until 1974 Sandringham was always the roof under which the Royal Family gathered for the Christmas celebrations. But as more children were born to the younger members of the family – and there are now up to forty relatives on the guest list – the huge house in Norfolk became just too small to accommodate the expanding family. Only Windsor Castle, with all its turrets, towers and hundreds of rooms, had sufficient space for everyone.

Sandringham, one of the Queen's private residences, was bought for the Prince of Wales (later King Edward VII) in the nineteenth century for the sum of £220,000 from the revenues of the Duchy of Cornwall, the traditional source of income for the Prince of Wales. It was then a very large house of 365 rooms, but the present Queen decided it was too expensive and impractical to maintain so many rooms and ordered 91 to be demolished. The family now only occupy a small part of the main building, which has comfortable but fairly cramped accommodation.

A royal Christmas has to have space for nannies, chefs, dressers, pages, footmen, policemen and valets, to name but a few. The Royal Family always travel with all their home comforts . . . which means an enormous amount of accommodation has to be found. Sandringham, of course, has its own resident domestic staff, and when the Queen first took the court to Windsor for Christmas the move caused great disappointment to the Sandringham retainers. But since the Royal Family dislike change, and old royal habits die hard, Her Majesty worked out a compromise. Normally, she herself leaves Buckingham Palace for Windsor on 22 December, and by Christmas Eve all the cousins, aunts, uncles and offspring are settled in at Windsor Castle. But by New Year's Day the immediate Royal family have packed up Christmas bag and baggage and moved on to Sandringham – where, on New Year's Day, they have a second Christmas, with turkey, plum pudding and passing the port all over again. So for royalty Christmas comes not once, but twice a year.

And though the routine may be upset while Windsor Castle gets its handsome old face lifted, Christmas will be back to normal service as soon as possible. And at least for a year or two the staff will not have the complicated task of transporting Christmas across country. The Christmas cards, every last bit of Christmas cake, fruits and chocolates will already be at Sandringham. The Royal Family are not superstitious about Twelfth Night, and Christmas lasts right through until every nut and chocolate has been eaten, and the Christmas cards, displayed on old-fashioned wooden clothes horses, are tired and dusty.

But first things first. For royalty, just like the rest of us, it's a time for buying presents, but with rather less hassle since they don't have to plod around crowded shops themselves. At one time, in less dangerous days, the Queen did her Christmas shopping at Harrods. Once this amazing emporium, which of course holds the royal warrant, had shut up shop to the general public in the evening, the Queen would discreetly appear, enter a side door from one of her Daimler cars, and set about enjoying the most marvellous shopping spree. It was a great treat for her; normally she never sees the inside of a store. But today security problems, mostly caused by the IRA, have meant that this one shopping outing a year is a pleasure that the Queen has to forego.

So now the shop comes to her. About three weeks before Christmas a gift-shop owner brings his wares to the Palace. He arrives in a laden estate car at the side door, and with the Palace staff coping with the fetching and carrying an enormous selection of goodies, mostly pretty artefacts for the home, is taken to the White Drawing

Room. Everything is laid out on trestle tables, prices marked and ready for the Queen's inspection. The Queen does her shopping every night after she has eaten dinner, and she makes an unhurried selection, choosing something for each and every one of her large family.

Public shopping, of course, is not easy for any of the Royal Family, though some manage to get away with it. Princess Diana adores Harrods and Harvey Nichols and the entire Knightsbridge shopping area, and she contrives to get there in person more often than you'd think.

And the Royal Family do keep Christmas in mind all year round. Another rich source of presents for these people who have everything are country craft fairs which take place in the summer. Spot a royal at one of these, and the chances are that they are doing a bit of Christmas shopping. These fairs, run by country landowners, are not your common or garden fair. Along with the cattle show, some of London's most glamorous stores show their wares. Asprey's are usually on parade along with Purdey's hideously expensive guns, and these are perfect places for top-class saddlers to show their wares. The green wellie brigade are out in force, buying. This up-market kind of country fair is one of the few places where Prince Charles, who hasn't been in a shop for years, actually gets to do a bit of shopping.

The family do of course have an enormous number of presents to buy. No one must be left out. And it's each member of the family's individual staff who sort it all out. Pages and footmen and valets all ring each other up asking: 'What does your one want?' Surprisingly, the choices are often pretty pedestrian. Prince Charles once bought his sister, Princess Anne, a doormat. But then she had asked for one. The Royal Family's needs are surprisingly simple. It is very rare for anyone to be given an expensive piece of jewellery or silver. This is a family that really has everything, built up over many generations as their ancestors augmented the royal jewel collection and added to their gallery of masterpieces by presents to each other. Today the list is more likely to contain place mats or calling trays (a tray with a complete breakfast set for serving breakfasts to guests). This item is always a winner with the Queen Mother who is a great believer in breakfast in bed. The men like accessories for their outdoor life – shooting jackets, or bits and pieces to go with the royal passion for picnics.

The Queen's shopping list is the longest, as she has the hundred or so staff to consider as well as her family. The housekeeper is in charge of staff gifts, and she begins organizing things as early as July. She will make a list of every employee, and the heads of the various Palace departments are given a separate list containing all their staff's names so they can ask what people would like. There is a rough budget of around £15 a head, though the price of each gift is eventually decided on length of service. The Queen spends more on a housemaid who has been in her service for many years than on a brand-new head chef. The long-serving staff often choose to have good china or cutlery and build up a service over the years. In the homes of most retired staff pride of place is given to a cabinet which houses the fine china that they have received each and every Christmas of their royal service. The housekeeper copes with the mammoth shopping spree involved, buying from the Army and Navy store at Victoria, which Buckingham Palace regard as their 'corner shop'.

For those who work at Buckingham Palace, Christmas begins when they receive an invitation from the Master of the Household. Sent on behalf of the monarch, it commands attendance at the Queen's staff party – which has to be the grandest staff party in the world. It is held on either the Tuesday or the Thursday before the Palace closes down for Christmas, and this invitation comes every other year. The Queen has such a vast number of people in her employ that even the Buckingham Palace Ballroom would become too crowded if everyone were asked at once, particularly as each employee is allowed to bring a guest – though it is now stipulated that the guest must be of the opposite sex. For a while there seemed to be rather a lot of males! Even the chefs get the day of the party off: the catering is done by Joe Lyons. The entire Palace is brilliantly lit and the state rooms are opened up. Everyone wears formal dress and the Royal Family mix in with their guests.

This is *the* night of the year for royal staff, and on 22 December, the day before the Queen and the court leave Buckingham Palace, they line up to be taken into the Bow Room. There the Queen waits to shake their hands and give each one their present. This duty done, the Queen leaves and Buckingham Palace closes down for the next three months.

The rest of the family join her later – at lunchtime on Christmas Eve. As soon as the smallest members of the family arrive they start putting up some of their own Christmas decorations (see p. 79). Each royal or family group of royals will come in their own chauffeur-driven transport. The limo is usually followed by another vehicle – a Land Rover or small van full of brightly wrapped presents. It is the staff's task to get all these parcels into the drawing room where the present-giving takes place. There are literally miles of corridors in Windsor, and quite enough at Sandringham, too, so there's competition to borrow trolleys from the kitchen staff on which to push the parcels from each guest's quarters through to the drawing room.

Following the Danish tradition which Queen Alexandra brought to England, the Royal Family exchange presents on Christmas Eve. In the glow from hundreds of lights on a twenty-foot Christmas tree, felled in the Sandringham woods and topped with a huge silver star, the royals gather behind closed doors to see what Santa has brought them. All the parcels are placed down the left-hand side of the room on tables covered with snowy-white linen cloths. The Queen's gifts are placed first, then Prince Charles's – everything is laid out in order of precedence. The children's presents are put separately around the foot of the tree.

The presents are opened with much tearing of expensive wrapping paper, and much the same squeals of delight common to any family can be heard. The only difference is that the royals don't have to clear up their own abandoned wrappings and string. The staff do that discreetly and quietly after everyone has gone into dinner.

The world received a fascinating glimpse of how the Royal Family relate to each other when, after she had left royal service, a house-maid produced for publication a collection of the gift tags with which the Royal Family had labelled their individual gifts. No doubt the Queen was not amused to see her gift labels printed in the *Sunday Express*, but we did learn that in the confines of the family Princess

Alexandra is known as The Pud, or Puddy; Prince Michael of Kent is Maou; Lord Nicholas Windsor, younger son of the Duke and Duchess of Kent, is Pooh; and Lady Gabriella Windsor, daughter of Prince and Princess Michael of Kent, is Phub. The Queen's children call her Mummy; to her son-in-law and daughters-in-law she is Ma'am. The Queen signs her gifts from Lilibet, her pet name. Only the Queen Mother is always, regally, Elizabeth R.

The real reason for Christmas is not forgotten. The Queen always goes to the midnight service on Christmas Eve, and again on Christmas morning. And while royalty prays, the chefs are hard at work in the kitchens where they have been since dawn.

They cook at least twenty-four turkeys for five separate meal sittings. The junior staff are served first, at eleven-thirty, at tables decorated with crackers, novelties and all the traditional trimmings. Then they go back to their duties and the senior staff sit down at midday. At a quarter to one it's time for nursery lunch for any very small royals, which gives the royal parents time to see their offspring before they go to their own lunch at one-fifteen.

The head chef joins the Royal Family in the dining room, where he carves the turkey with style and ceremony. Apart from the moment when the Queen hands him his Christmas present, this is the only time in the year when he will see his employer. The junior staff wait at table, and, having had their own lunch, they are sometimes a little merry. Each man will have had a large whisky or gin, and the women a glass of port. Everyone will also have been given a glass of wine with their turkey, and if the merriment shows, as it frequently does, the Queen turns a blind eye.

The State Dining Room where the Queen eats is not decorated with streamers or balloons, but is beautifully and tastefully Christmas-like with banks and banks of superb poinsettias and cyclamens from the royal nurseries. This is the only time in the year when there are chocolates on the table, along with the sugar-coated almonds that the Queen loves. There are crackers to pull, but though the younger members of the family may don paper hats, the Queen does not. Even in the privacy of her own dining room and surrounded by her family, a paper hat would demean the dignity of the monarchy. If the Queen wears anything on her head when she eats it is a tiara.

The staff get tomato soup as a starter, the Queen and her guests a lobster dish. From then on the royal lunch is the same as our lunch – turkey, little chipolata sausages, two veg and roast potatoes for all, followed, of course, by the chef's Christmas pudding. And it has to be over by three so that everyone can watch the Queen's speech on television. Only then do the remaining kitchen staff get to eat their Christmas lunch.

Very sensibly, everyone takes a walk after lunch – if only to make room for the next meal. Tea is served with an enormous iced cake which has been made weeks before by the pastry chef. It's probably a relief that after tea there is a little 'free time' for those who want to snooze, walk, take a bath or play board games. And by eight-fifteen everyone is eating yet again – a candlelit meal, usually of lamb. Elsewhere, the staff are given cold meats traditionally presented around a magnificent glazed and decidedly bad-tempered looking boar's head. Supper over, a mind-bendingly noisy disco is laid on for them.

When the children were young, the Royal Family liked to play charades. They still play, but Diana, Fergie and Princess Margaret's children, Viscount Linley and Lady Sarah Armstrong-Jones, now organize a disco of their own. They roll back the carpet and, with one of them acting as disc jockey, dance into the early hours. They sometimes wear silly masks and present their own cabaret, and one year Diana wore a pair of very large plastic breasts while she, Fergie and Andrew tried to 'debag' Prince Charles. Normally rather reserved, the Prince of Wales entered into the spirit of the occasion and chased the girls round the room. Whether the heir to the throne actually managed to keep his trousers on is not recorded.

Boxing Day is devoted to shooting – unless, of course, it falls on a Sunday. With Prince Philip in charge, the men are out with the dogs for a typical shooting day. It's a break for the staff, who have their own little parties until they have to be back on duty when the Royal Family return, ravenous, as dusk falls.

The royals are consistent in their enjoyment of all things traditional. Their Christmas, though grander, compares with the

Christmas enjoyed by most of their subjects. And so, indeed, does their Easter. This, too, is normally a Windsor festival which might now have to take place at either Sandringham or Balmoral. But one thing is certain – whichever of their many houses the family visit, their Easter routine won't vary by a hair's breadth from that of last year, the year before, or ten years before that.

At nine-thirty breakfast will be served and Prince Philip will preside over a table surrounded by his children and his grand-children (see p. 30). The Queen Mother will be upstairs having her breakfast in bed. The royals' traditional free-range Easter boiled egg is served with fresh bread, butter and honey. And after breakfast there will be a little exchange of Easter gifts, though never anything particularly expensive. Usually they give small pretty presents like the hand-painted bone china boxes with hinged lids which Princess Diana collects. They are made in the West Country by Crummels, and at present she has a collection of over twenty-five, scattered on tables and shelves in her sitting room.

The chef makes hot cross buns on Good Friday and the Queen goes to church, but unlike at Christmas there is no set time for the family to gather. The Queen always escapes from Buckingham Palace on Maundy Thursday, immediately after she has completed the annual ceremony of the presentation of Maundy Money. Those who decide to join her for Easter drift in when they feel so inclined, usually some time on Good Friday, but it is not obligatory to do so. Even so, the immediate family are always present. Princess Margaret, the Queen's children and their spouses would be most unlikely not to come. But other royalty may prefer to spend Easter at their own homes. The Queen Mother is most certainly with her family. She leaves her own home, Royal Lodge, in Windsor Great Park to stay with her daughter, but returns to Royal Lodge for the rest of the six-week Easter court.

In the normal way, over the four days of Easter all meals are served in the Queen's private dining room. This sounds as if it might be small and intimate, but it is not. Situated on the first floor of the Queen's Tower, it overlooks the East Terrace of the castle. The walls are covered in gold damask which sets off a fine collection of military paintings. The ceilings are high and ornate, and the windows look out over the golfcourse with Heathrow and London in the distance.

During this Easter visit, the East Terrace is open to the public, and after lunch the Queen leads her family into the Green Drawing Room next door. There, they sit and listen to the band play and watch the world go by. With a bit of luck, the public can get a quick glimpse of them before they disappear back into the bowels of the castle.

The cheerful music from the band has always been a favourite of Prince Charles. 'One thing about this job,' he once said, 'is that you do get your own private orchestra a lot of the time.'

Easter at Windsor signals the start of the polo season for Prince Charles, and, weather permitting, he will be playing his first match of the year at Smith's Lawn no matter which home houses the Easter court. Windsor has a helicopter pad, put in by the restless Duke of Edinburgh so that he could come and go without any problems. If Prince Charles comes to Windsor from another royal home for his polo in the next few years, that is undoubtedly where he will land.

It is during the Easter court that the Queen celebrates her real birthday, 21 April. On this real birthday (as opposed to her official one) she and the Duke generally slip away together. They are flown on an Andover of the Queen's Flight to Norfolk. They leave from Heathrow, and everyone at the castle knows when Her Majesty is on her way. The plane flies right by the Queen's Tower at Windsor. Forty minutes later they land and are driven to Wood Farm, a small house on the Sandringham estate. She likes to stay here for two days, inspecting her stud farm and the new foals born in the spring. Those who know her well say that these two days are some of the happiest of her year.

In May, reluctantly, the Queen returns to Buckingham Palace. The Easter court is over, and duty calls.

Here are some of the dishes served at celebratory royal meals:

ROAST TURKEY WITH LEMON AND PARSLEY STUFFING

RICH CHRISTMAS CAKE

CAULIFLOWER AND CORIANDER SOUP

SPINACH TERRINE WITH TOMATO COULIS

HOT CROSS BUNS

CHOCOLATE TRUFFLES

ROAST TURKEY WITH LEMON AND PARSLEY STUFFING

1 plump 7–8 lb (3–3.5 kg) turkey
2 oz (60 g) butter
6 rashers fat bacon
6 oz (175 g) fresh white breadcrumbs
½ onion, chopped
½ oz (15 g) parsley, chopped
Rind of 1 large lemon, grated finely
3 oz (90 g) butter, melted
1 large egg, beaten

Pre-heat the oven to 220°C/425°F/gas mark 7. Remove giblets and neck from the turkey if necessary. Spread the butter over the breast and legs and lay the bacon rashers on top. Cover the breast with a piece of foil or buttered greaseproof paper. Combine the breadcrumbs, onion, parsley and lemon rind and stir in the melted butter and beaten egg. Use to stuff the rear and the neck of the turkey just before roasting. Place the turkey in a large roasting tin and roast for 3–3½ hours, basting frequently. Leave to rest for 15 minutes before serving.

RICH CHRISTMAS CAKE

This rich fruit cake has the advantage of keeping in perfect condition for up to a year – if anything it improves the longer it is kept. For the busy Palace cooks this saves them a lot of time during the hectic run-up to Christmas.

1 lb (450 g) butter
12 oz (350 g) caster sugar
1 tablespoon treacle
10 eggs
1¼ lb (600 g) plain flour
4 oz (125 g) ground almonds
1 teaspoon ground nutmeg
1 teaspoon ground mixed spice
1 teaspoon salt
1 lb (450 g) sultanas
1 lb (450 g) raisins
4 oz (125 g) glacé cherries
4 oz (125 g) candied peel
1 teaspoon almond essence
3 tablespoons brandy

Pre-heat the oven to 150°C/300°F/gas mark 2. Cream the butter and sugar together until light and fluffy. Add the treacle and drop in the eggs one at a time, alternating with a tablespoon of sieved flour mixed with the almonds, spices and salt. Beat well after each addition. Add the fruit, the essence and the brandy and mix well together. Line a 12-inch (30-cm) cake tin with greased paper, fill with the cake mixture and bake for 2–3 hours or until a skewer comes out clean. Cover with marzipan and royal icing as usual.

CAULIFLOWER AND CORIANDER SOUP

A fresh and creamy soup that is the perfect start to a light lunch over a festive period marked by rich meals. With fresh rolls and butter and perhaps a green salad, it makes a meal in itself.

2 oz (60 g) butter
1 medium cauliflower, broken into florets
1 potato, diced
1 onion, chopped
1 pint (600 ml) chicken stock or water
1 pint (600 ml) milk
1 teaspoon ground coriander
Salt and pepper
Parsley for garnish
A little cream to serve

Melt the butter in a large saucepan. Sweat the vegetables in the butter, covered, for 5 minutes until they begin to soften. Stir in the stock or water, milk, coriander and seasoning and bring to the boil. Lower the heat and simmer for 30 minutes or until the vegetables are tender. Puree or blend the soup to a smooth cream and serve with a swirl of cream sprinkled with parsley.

SPINACH TERRINE WITH TOMATO COULIS

The Prince and Princess of Wales eat sparingly and lightly and much prefer vegetables to the richness of meat. Here is a recipe which is healthy, light and attractive with its pleasant contrast of the speckled green terrine and the vivid tomato sauce.

Serves 4 as a main course, 6 as a starter
1 lb (450 g) spinach, fresh chopped or frozen
4 eggs, beaten
¼ pint (150 ml) double cream
2 oz (60 g) Cheddar cheese, grated
2 oz (60 g) Parmesan cheese, freshly grated
1 sprig fresh basil, chopped
Salt and pepper to taste
1 lb (450 g) tomatoes
1 onion, sliced
Olive oil for frying

Pre-heat the oven to 220°C/425°F/gas mark 7. Mix together the spinach, eggs, cream, cheeses, basil and a little salt and pepper. Divide the mixture among individual buttered soufflé dishes and stand in a baking tray of water to come two-thirds of the way up the side of the dishes. Place in the oven for 30 minutes or until set. Leave to cool overnight.

To make the sauce, peel the tomatoes and remove the pips (the tomatoes can be sieved). Sweat the onion in a little olive oil until soft, then add the tomatoes and simmer gently for 10 minutes. Pour into a serving dish and chill. Just before serving, turn out the spinach terrines on to the tomato sauce and serve with a separate vinaigrette dressing.

By Royal Invitation

HOT CROSS BUNS

No Easter weekend is complete without a fragrant hot cross bun served warm from the oven with plenty of fresh, cold butter.

Makes 6 buns
Just under ¼ pint (150 ml) milk
Just under ¼ pint (150 ml) water
1 level tablespoon dried yeast
1 lb (450 g) strong bread flour
1 teaspoon salt
1 teaspoon ground mixed spice
½ teaspoon ground mixed cinnamon
1 oz (25 g) caster sugar
3 oz (90 g) currants
1 oz (25 g) butter, melted
1 egg, beaten
A little sugar and water to glaze

Heat the milk and water to hand-hot and sprinkle the dried yeast on top. Stir, and leave in a warm place until frothy. Sieve the flour, salt and spices into a bowl and mix with the sugar and fruit. Add the butter, egg and yeast mixture to the flour and mix to a rough dough. Turn on to a floured surface and knead until the dough becomes smooth and no longer sticky. Shape into a ball, return it to the bowl and place inside a large, greased polythene bag. Leave in a warm place to rise until it has doubled in size (about 1½ hours). Turn the dough out and knock all the air bubbles out by kneading vigorously. Divide into individual buns, place on a greased tray and cut a small cross in the top of each one. Place inside the polythene bag again for 30 minutes. Pre-heat the oven to 220°C/425°F/gas mark 7. Dissolve a little sugar and water together, and just before baking brush this liquid over the buns. Bake for 20 minutes. To test if they are cooked, rap the bottom of one and it should sound hollow.

CHOCOLATE TRUFFLES

Makes 20–24 truffles
6 oz (175 g) icing sugar
1 oz (25 g) cocoa powder
1 tablespoon single cream
1 tablespoon rum
2 oz (60 g) butter
2 tablespoons cocoa powder and 1 tablespoon icing sugar for dusting

Sift the icing sugar and cocoa into a bowl. In another bowl beat the cream, rum and butter together until soft and creamy. Mix into the sugar and cocoa. Shape the truffle mixture into small balls and roll them in the dusting ingredients. Place in little petit fours cases and chill. Keep any that are not eaten immediately in the fridge.

SHORT BIBLIOGRAPHY

1 Aubery, Ronald, *A Royal Chef's Notebook*, Gresham Books, 1978
2 Burnet, Sir Alistair, *In Private In Public, The Prince and Princess of Wales*, O'Mara Books, 1986
3 Kingston, Patrick, *Royal Trains*, David & Charles Ltd, 1985
4 McDowell, Colin, *A Hundred Years of Royal Style*, Century Hutchinson, 1987
5 McKee, Mrs, *The Royal Cookery Book*, Arlington Books, 1983
6 Massingberd, Hugh Montgomery, *Her Majesty The Queen*, Antler Books, 1985
7 Oliver, Charles, *Dinner at Buckingham Palace*, Prentice-Hall Inc, 1972
8 Parker, Eileen, *Step Aside For Royalty*, Bachman & Turner, 1982
9 Talbot, Godfrey, *The Country Life Book of Queen Elizabeth, The Queen Mother*, Country Life Books, 1978
10 Young, Sheila, *The Queen's Jewellery*, Ebury Press, 1968

INDEX